Cambridge Elements

Elements in Metaphysics
edited by
Tuomas E. Tahko
University of Bristol

SOCIAL ONTOLOGY

Brian Epstein
Tufts University

Shaftesbury Road, Cambridge CB2 8EA, United Kingdom

One Liberty Plaza, 20th Floor, New York, NY 10006, USA

477 Williamstown Road, Port Melbourne, VIC 3207, Australia

314–321, 3rd Floor, Plot 3, Splendor Forum, Jasola District Centre, New Delhi – 110025, India

103 Penang Road, #05–06/07, Visioncrest Commercial, Singapore 238467

Cambridge University Press is part of Cambridge University Press & Assessment, a department of the University of Cambridge.

We share the University's mission to contribute to society through the pursuit of education, learning and research at the highest international levels of excellence.

www.cambridge.org
Information on this title: www.cambridge.org/9781009663243
DOI: 10.1017/9781009290562

© Brian Epstein 2025

This publication is in copyright. Subject to statutory exception and to the provisions of relevant collective licensing agreements, with the exception of the Creative Commons version the link for which is provided below, no reproduction of any part may take place without the written permission of Cambridge University Press & Assessment.

An online version of this work is published at doi.org/10.1017/9781009290562 under a Creative Commons Open Access license CC-BY-NC 4.0 which permits re-use, distribution and reproduction in any medium for non-commercial purposes providing appropriate credit to the original work is given and any changes made are indicated. To view a copy of this license visit https://creativecommons.org/licenses/by-nc/4.0

When citing this work, please include a reference to the DOI 10.1017/9781009290562

First published 2025

A catalogue record for this publication is available from the British Library

ISBN 978-1-009-66324-3 Hardback
ISBN 978-1-009-29054-8 Paperback
ISSN 2633-9862 (online)
ISSN 2633-9854 (print)

Cambridge University Press & Assessment has no responsibility for the persistence or accuracy of URLs for external or third-party internet websites referred to in this publication and does not guarantee that any content on such websites is, or will remain, accurate or appropriate.

Social Ontology

Elements in Metaphysics

DOI: 10.1017/9781009290562
First published online: April 2025

Brian Epstein
Tufts University
Author for correspondence: Brian Epstein, brian.epstein@tufts.edu

Abstract: Social ontology is the study of the nature of the social world. This Element aims to provide an overview of this burgeoning field and also to map the questions that theories in social ontology address. When we encounter a theory of some social thing – groups, law, gender, and so on – how are we to read it? What classes of theories have been explored and abandoned, and what classes are new and promising? The Element distinguishes theories of *social construction* from theories that characterize the *products* of social construction. For each, the Element works through a "toy" theory and then discusses features that more realistic theories ought to include. Three running examples are discussed throughout the Element: (1) property, or ownership; (2) race, or racialized kinds; (3) collective attitudes (i.e., beliefs, desires, knowledge, intentions, etc., of groups and organizations). This title is also available as Open Access on Cambridge Core.

This Element also has a video abstract:
www.cambridge.org/EMPH_Epstein_abstract

Keywords: social construction, race, ontology, social theory, collective action

© Brian Epstein 2025

ISBNs: 9781009663243 (HB), 9781009290548 (PB), 9781009290562 (OC)
ISSNs: 2633-9862 (online), 2633-9854 (print)

Contents

1 Introduction   1

2 Structuring the Inquiry   9

3 Two Other Cases   23

4 Social Construction: A Simple Theory   28

5 Developing a Theory of Social Construction   36

6 Characterizing Social Kinds: Starting Simple   45

7 Ways to Characterize Social Kinds   51

8 Pulling It Together: Social Kinds and Social Construction   67

    References   72

1 Introduction

Social ontology is the study of the nature of the social world. "What is X?" social ontology asks, where 'X' stands for any social thing whatever.

What, for instance, are groups? What are corporations? What is law? What is race? What is gender? What is language? Fill in a social object, a social kind, a social category – and it's a topic for social ontology. Even more general questions are in its purview as well: What is society? What is the social? What, for that matter, is a "what is X" question?

The aim of this Element is to provide some structure to this burgeoning field – to map the questions that theories in social ontology ask, as well as the sorts of answers given to them. When we encounter a theory of some social thing – groups, law, gender, and so on – how are we to read it? How should we compare this theory to competing theories? What classes of theories have been explored and abandoned, and what classes are new and promising? How might we build new theories without reinventing the wheel?

In a sense, social ontology is among the oldest fields of philosophy. Even before Socrates, philosophers including Protagoras, Antiphon, Heraclitus, and Euthyphro argued over the nature and sources of justice, ethics, and language. Some held they were a product of nature, some of human agreement, and some held they were a product of agreement of the gods. But inquiries into the nature of the social have, at least in the last century, been fragmented. And at times, sidelined: in the early to mid-twentieth century, it was out of fashion (at least in analytic philosophy) to study the "nature of things" altogether, and even with the rebirth of metaphysics in the late twentieth century, the social was never central to philosophical concerns. (I remember that in the "metaphysics core" seminar I took as a graduate student, the professor commented on the first day that there are only two live topics in metaphysics: causation and universals. In retrospect, seems bizarre.)

Today, the situation has changed. While theorists working in social ontology still take radically different perspectives from one another, the field is beginning to coalesce, with people talking with one another across disciplines, and interest in the social surging. Inquiries into the nature of groups, social cognition, law, race, gender, economics, and so on are starting to inform one another. Diverse social phenomena sometimes exhibit common features. And sometimes they bring out differences, breaking down the assumption that one's favorite theory or case study is the key to understanding all the social world.

To map the field, it is a help to consider particular cases, keeping in mind all their complexity. I will use three running examples through the Element: (1) Property, or ownership; (2) Race, or racialized kinds; (3) Collective attitudes (i.e., beliefs, desires, knowledge, intentions, etc., of groups and organizations). It is, of course, possible that any (or all) of these things is a mistake or illusion. Perhaps races do not exist. Perhaps group actions or intentions are just a loose way of speaking. But these cases are useful, in different ways, for mapping out various questions and answers in the field. I start with property.

1.1 The Case of Property

Discussions in social ontology can be annoyingly abstract, so let us begin with a case that has real-world consequences.

In 1992, the High Court of Australia handed down a landmark decision in the case of *Mabo vs. Queensland No. 2*. The case provided the legal basis, for the first time since the British began to colonize New South Wales in the 1780s, for indigenous people to claim native title rights over land and waters in Australia.

The case was brought by Eddie Mabo and other members of the Meriam people, who had lived on Mer Island since before British colonization. The state of Queensland argued that there never had been native title over the land. Furthermore, they claimed, even if native peoples once had title, it had been removed by successive legislative acts.[1] To decide *Mabo*, the court considered the historical and current practices of the islanders – the fact that they had long built permanent structures along the coastline, named and recognized villages, and followed long-standing customs and practices regarding who was to live where.

The 1992 decision denied that Australia was practically unoccupied prior to James Cook's arrival – a doctrine known as "terra nullius" – and rejected the claim that its inhabitants lacked fixed connections to the land or settled law.[2] And therefore ruled that there could be native title.

The *Mabo* decision probably served the interests of justice.[3] But its reasoning raises as many questions as it answers. For someone to have title over a piece of land – that is, for land to be a person's property – the court requires that certain conditions be met. In particular, that there are systems of law and land tenure in place, as well as a continuous history of occupying and using the land. But are these conditions correct? And according to whose conception of law?

Or suppose that, according to British common law, Meriam practices did *not* count as settled law. Would it then be appropriate to *deny* them title? How and why

---

[1] Including the Queensland Land Act 1910 and the Queensland Coast Islands Declaratory Act 1985.
[2] The court in *Milirrpum v Nabalco Pty Ltd* (1971) uses similar reasoning, referencing Yolŋu's "subtle and elaborate" system of law.
[3] Although, as implemented and codified, particularly in the form of the Native Title Act of 1993 and subsequent amendments, it has done little to remediate inequities.

do fixed connections to the land figure into the determination of title, especially communal title? And why should the conditions for ownership in British common law be themselves legitimate for the proper assignment of title?[4]

To at least some extent, these questions – questions about justice and the redistribution of property, about what the law is and should be regarding property, about the facts about who owned what and when – involve the *nature* of property. What is property? What does it take to establish that a piece of land is the property of a person or of a community? Is property natural, conventional, customary, institutional, structural, economically determined, or perhaps a mass illusion?

These questions matter for practical purposes. In current Australian law, for instance, there is a twelve-part test for establishing native title. Many of these parts aim at establishing *facts* of ownership. (Other parts aim at identifying the eligibility of claimants, where the claimants are often groups rather than individuals. This too involves questions of the nature of social entities.) How the legal system chooses to assess the facts of ownership depends on prevailing theories of what ownership consists in.

It would be a mistake to overinflate the relevance of philosophy, in a context like this. Legal views on native title are as much about posturing and power politics as they are about seeking the facts. Still, if one is to criticize lawyers and legislators on this basis, then one is at least somewhat committed to the idea that there *are* genuine property rights, that property has been misappropriated, and that the law can get it wrong. And maybe total cynicism is not warranted: at least some players do seem to be moved by what they believe to be the truth about ownership and justice.

Even if property itself is an outgrowth of the exercise of power, *that* is a theory of the nature of property, one that bears on how debates ought to go. Even if one holds property to be a fabrication, or to be a tool of an oppressive ideology, those too are claims about its nature.

1.2 Inquiring into the Nature of Property

If someone is interested in the nature of property, they might read a history of the development of property. They might read an anthropology of cultural

---

[4] Unsurprisingly, the actual facts about the appropriation of land in the New South Wales colony involve at least as much politics and judgments of power as they do legal bases. It is often claimed that James Cook declared New South Wales terra nullius, but that seems likely to be incorrect. (The term is a late nineteenth-century coinage, so he surely did not use that term, but the idea is an older one. Still, it seems not to have been the basis on which claims of ownership by the crown were based.) It is a complicated story how genuine legal concerns, legal rationalizations, political judgments, and raw exercises of power played into the different ways title was assigned in Australia and other colonial contexts. See Attwood (2020).

differences and universals regarding property. They might read a handbook of property law. They might read an intellectual history of theories of property. They might read economic theories of the functions of property. They might read a Marxist critique of the social structures based on property relations. They might read a text in political theory on just or legitimate notions of property. Which of these, if any, is an effective route to inquire into property's nature – that is, into what property is?

An encouraging – albeit daunting – answer is that they are all pertinent. Theorists in all these areas often explore and contribute to ontology. But, of course, they each have other concerns as well. Not *every* aspect of the history of property is pertinent to an inquiry into its nature. Not every detail of a culture's practices, a state's administration, or an ethical consequence is pertinent either. How should we understand which inquiries are "ontological," and how can we sort them out from all the others?

To see how an *ontological* inquiry might go, we do not need to confine ourselves to the recent metaphysics literature, but can find informative discussions going back centuries. In fact, some early modern theorizing about property nicely structures the problem. A particularly impressive example is the fourth book of Samuel von Pufendorf's 1672 work *On the Law of Nature and Nations*, which is dedicated to the nature of property. It is worth a minute to consider its approach.

Pufendorf's discussion can be divided into three topics:

(I) A theory of what property "proceeds from" (chapters 1–4)
(II) The conditions for a property relation to hold between a person and a thing (chapters 5–7 and 9–12)
(III) The norms associated with property (chapters 8 and 13)

Much of the discussion covers topic (II), and Pufendorf emphasizes that different societies have different conditions for ownership. For instance, while some things – like the open ocean – just do not make sense as property, some societies allow national ownership of certain parts of the sea, while other societies do not. Similarly, different societies have different conditions for the "original possession" of animals: in some societies, an animal captured on another person's land to be the possession of the capturer, while in others, it is the possession of the landowner.[5]

---

[5] Interestingly, he does not speak of differences among norms associated with property: rather, he says that these arise from the nature of ownership. "Now that we have inquired into the origin and nature of dominion, and into the ways in which it is constituted, our next task is to consider the obligations which immediately and on their own account come to men upon the introduction of dominion over things" (Pufendorf, Book IV, Ch. 13, Sec. 1).

All this ties to the theory Pufendorf presents in topic (I). According to Pufendorf, property proceeds from tacit agreement: this is in contrast to a view like Locke's, where property proceeds from God's endowment of shared ownership of the world, together with self-ownership. Since tacit agreements can differ from society to society, the conditions for something to be owned can differ from society to society as well.

In the next section, I will look more at Pufendorf's structure, especially the separation of topic (I) from the other two.[6] For now, though, I only want to point out that this structure is clearly an inquiry into the *nature* of property, into *ontological* questions. Even when Pufendorf speaks of the "origin" of property, his aim is to give a theory of the ontological basis of property, not historical or causal ones. The theory is a theory of what property *is*.

Just because he aims at an ontological inquiry does not mean that he succeeds, nor that his way of structuring things is the right one. But it does bring out questions to help us embark on our own ontological inquiry. Are the conditions associated with x *owning* y part of the nature of ownership? Are there general conditions associated with the nature of property in general, having as instances the ownership relations in particular societies? What is it to give a theory of what property "proceeds from," and what is the idea behind his saying that it "*immediately* arises" from agreement? Is there a difference between that and the practical explanation for making such agreements? Are the norms associated with property part of its nature, or do they derive from its nature? These are at least the sorts of questions we might organize and address in a theory of the nature of property.

1.3 Some Aims of Social Ontology

Stepping back from the case of property, what do we mean to accomplish in studying the nature of the social world? Unsurprisingly, different theorists in the field aim at very different things, some at odds with one another. It is not even accurate to say that all theorists in social ontology aim to uncover the nature of social entities, since some will deny that there are objective facts of the matter about what social entities are, and some that the idea of things having "natures" is ill-conceived.

Still, we can identify a range of aims that motivate many theorists in the field. Here are some of the top ones:

(1) Demystify the Social via Ontological Reduction or Explanation

According to many theorists, social entities are not "fundamental" things in the world, but rather are the products of other things. And hence are in need

---

[6] Although Pufendorf presents this inquiry clearly, he is not the first to separate things in this way.

of explanation. Property and ownership, for instance, are not basic or primitive features of objects, but rather are the products of social interactions of one sort or other. An intention or belief of a corporation is not a primitive feature of the world, but again is the product of some sort of social interaction.

An aim of many social ontologists, therefore, is to demystify the social in the sense of explaining social phenomena in terms of other phenomena. The simplest versions of this take the form of "individualistic" explanations or reductions of social phenomena, that is, in terms of nonsocial features of individual people. So, for instance, a theorist might argue the following: Group G has belief B if and only if all the members of G individually believe B. That is a kind of "reductive" account of group belief. (Not a very good account, but this is just a simple illustration.)

Many theoretical accounts in social ontology aim at a sort of philosophical "naturalism." Whether or not they are meant to be reductive, their idea is to explain either particular social phenomena or social phenomena in general in terms that fit them into the natural order.

(2) Revalue the Social, or Rethink What It Is to Be Social

A different aim – perhaps in opposition to the previous one – is to re-center the social in our conception of the nature of the world. Some theorists argue that social groups or features of groups are ontologically distinctive in some way. One view, for instance, is that groups are "plural subjects," just as individuals are individual subjects. Some go on to hold that groups have beliefs, desires, and other attitudes that are analogous to – rather than derivative on – the beliefs, desires, and other attitudes of individual people.

Other theorists flip the determination relation holding between social things and individuals: for instance, instead of holding that social groups are determined by individuals interacting with one another, they hold that individual people are themselves socially constituted. Or that human action is determined as much by social structures as by the activity of individuals.

Some such theorists are opposed to "naturalizing" the social world, while others aim to expand our conception of what it is to naturalize.

(3) Contribute to Other Fields That Work with Social Entities

A different aim of social ontology is practical: to contribute to other fields, especially to other areas of philosophy and to the social sciences. Collective responsibility, for instance, is an important philosophical inquiry. When are groups, nations, or corporations to be held responsible for their actions? At least part of the question is what it *is* for groups, nations, and corporations to act.[7] And for them to believe, know, and intend. And for them to persist over time. All of those are questions in social ontology that bear on theories of collective responsibility.

Likewise, an aim of some social ontologists is to contribute to the social sciences. At the heart of any discipline are conceptual distinctions and categorizations. And models, both qualitative and quantitative, involve the choice not only of causal factors a modeler finds to be significant, but also determinations of how parts of the world are composed by other parts. Some theorists hold that inquiry into the nature of social entities can contribute to these, while others are skeptical that the sciences can be informed by the incursions of philosophers.

(4) Critique and Improve Social Categories

Given that social entities are the products of social interaction, and different societies interact in different ways, it seems likely that the social categories and kinds we have are not the *only* way they could be. Different societies have different categories of property, and some have no such category at all. Different societies have different categories of race, and others have no such category at all. A number of theorists take social ontology to be, at least in part, in the service of social criticism, arguing that the social categories there actually are in a given society are not the way they must be.

One critical project involves "debunking" categories, showing that widespread beliefs about them are mistaken. Perhaps it is widely held, for instance, that property is an efficient solution to a coordination problem. That is, that property is generally understood as a rational device to improve outcomes to all actors given a particular kind of social problem. A debunking theorist might not dispute that reasoning in principle, but might argue that our institution of property bears little resemblance to the device described in that diagnosis. Instead, the debunker might argue that property in contemporary society is constructed so as to play a very different functional role; for instance, to support preexisting relations of inequality. The idea is to apply what Paul Ricoeur calls a "hermeneutics of suspicion" to important social categories. We cannot take the nature and purposes of various social phenomena at face value, but instead it is the job of social ontology to suspect that there are deeper and perhaps less savory explanations for them and aspects of their natures.

With this or another methodology, an inquiry into the nature of social entities provides a basis for criticizing them. Some projects are strictly negative, while others work to improve social categories.

---

[7] See Collins 2019.

Some also deny that there are correct or privileged descriptions of social phenomena. Instead, they propose that certain inquiries in social ontology require an "ameliorative" analysis.

(5) Apply and Improve Philosophical Tools

Philosophical work in recent decades has produced substantial innovations in analytical tools. We have a much clearer understanding of language, logic, cognition, functions, reduction, explanation, in addition to metaphysical notions like composition, constitution, and determination. Recent work in social ontology aims to draw on all of these, in order to improve our understanding of the social. But it also promises to return the favor. Many of the tools of metaphysics, for instance, have been developed with only a rudimentary look at social examples. Some social ontology has the aim of drawing on the social to understand how metaphysics more generally might look.

(6) Pursue a Project That Is Interesting for Its Own Sake

Social ontology is complicated and thorny, and improves from both broad and deep interdisciplinary exploration – technical, historical, scientific, sociological, and more. So it is endlessly fascinating. I find myself driven by this aim probably even more than by the others.

Skepticism about These Aims

The foundations and aims of social ontology are contested, and for every philosopher who advocates a project, there is one who denies its utility. Some reject common methods of social ontology, such as the application of analytic metaphysics to the field, or taking ascriptions of cognitive properties to groups seriously. Some reject a descriptive approach to the social world, while others insist on it. Some put critical projects at the center of the field, and others deny its critical utility. Some connect ontology to the practice of social science, while others dispute it.

1.4 Plan for the Element

As for this Element, my aim is to provide something of an overview of the field, but equally to map out some structure to inquiries in social ontology and see how theories that one might encounter or develop in the field can be understood and compared. As I mentioned, I will also consider some running cases – race and group attitudes, in addition to property.

In Section 2, I focus the discussion on social kinds, and present a framework for structuring inquiries into their nature. I distinguish theories of *social construction* from theories that characterize the *products* of social construction. In Section 3, I briefly present two other case studies: race and group attitudes. Section 4 presents a "toy" theory of social construction, to see how even a simple theory needs to be elaborated and what challenges it faces. Section 5 then considers varieties of theories of social construction more generally, and situates some existing theories to show how they might be understood. Section 6 presents a simple class of theories of the "products" of social construction, and in Section 7 I discuss different approaches to characterizing social kinds, where a theorist might provide more than or less than a set of necessary and sufficient conditions for membership in a kind. And then in Section 8 I draw the threads back together again – connecting social construction to the resulting social kinds.

This Element is short, but my aim is to give an overview of key questions regarding the nature of social entities, a way of understanding what many theorists are aiming at, and to structure and sketch different approaches one could take in the field.

2 Structuring the Inquiry

Our quick look at property gave us some suggestions as to how to start an ontological inquiry into a social phenomenon. But how do we develop a clear method we can use for this and other cases? And how can we situate and organize existing theories in the literature? My aim in this section is to develop this structure.

To begin with, we need to make a choice, to make our lives manageable. Social things come in many categories: social properties, social objects or particulars, social facts, social kinds, and so on. It would be unwieldy – and confusing – to theorize about all of these at once. And it would be even worse to leave it unspecified which we are targeting. We will spare ourselves a lot of frustration if we focus on particular targets.

So for the purposes of this Element, I will choose a target that is aligned with many (though not all) contemporary approaches to social ontology. Namely, to focus on *social kinds* as the target of our inquiry. I discuss this in Subsection 2.1.

Subsequently, I will discuss how – given this focus – we can structure our inquiry. Roughly speaking, the overall structure I propose is to divide it into two: one component is to explain the *construction* of social kinds, and the other is to *characterize* social kinds, that is, the *products* of construction. On some theories, these are separate, and on some, they overlap or even coincide. But even if they do coincide, it is helpful to look at the inquiry from both sides.

2.1 The Targets of the Inquiry

Social ontology casts a wide net: in addressing questions of the form "what is X?" it is fair game to fill in anything social for X. The problem is that it becomes a mess if we do not constrain the categories of things that X can be. Historically, different theorists have focused on different targets. Some theorists work with an ontology of *facts*: Émile Durkheim founded the field of sociology as the study of social facts. John Searle, in *The Construction of Social Reality*, theorizes about what he calls "institutional facts." I too work with an ontology of social facts in my book *The Ant Trap*. But there are many other ways to go. Others focus on social objects, social properties, social events, or social processes. It is increasingly widespread, though, to cast the inquiry in terms of *social kinds*.

In asking, "what is property," for instance, we are not talking about the nature of some particular thing that is owned, like a particular book or coffee machine or plot of land. Rather, we are talking about something general, something that people and plots of land are instances of. Similarly with other inquiries: we are interested in race, in gender, in beliefs as held by groups, and so on.

Natural Kinds

The idea of a social kind is largely understood in relation to *natural* kinds. The rough idea of a natural kind is this: although there are innumerable ways of categorizing things in the world, some ways are distinctive or privileged, and some not so much. We can stipulate entirely arbitrary groupings – like the one that includes this cat and that fork and Beethoven's ninth symphony. Groupings like those are presumably not natural or distinctive or privileged.

There are various ways that kinds might be distinctive or privileged. The idea of a *natural* kind is of a kind whose distinctiveness arises from *nature,* as opposed to from things like human stipulation or activity. Just what natural kinds are – what it is to be a kind and what it is to be natural – is contentious.[8] But natural kinds are widely understood to fit into scientific inquiry, and to be related to laws and inductive inference. They also are widely taken to play a key role in theories of reference, that is, of how certain words acquire the meanings they do.

Sparseness: That Natural and Social Kinds "Metaphysically Stick Out"

Natural kinds are sparse: most groupings do not correspond to natural kinds.[9] The kind *water* corresponds to things that are composed of H_2O, but *schwater* – which

---

[8] On natural kinds, see Bird and Tobin 2023, and on the history of natural kinds, see Magnus 2015.
[9] I say "corresponds to" because I do not want to assume that a kind is identical to a grouping of things.

corresponds to everything composed of H_2O plus all cats and all silver salad forks – is not a natural kind. Perhaps the way to understand this is that there *is* no kind *schwater*, that is, that the kind *water* exists and *schwater* does not. Or perhaps it is that *schwater* is a kind, but merely a *nominal* one.[10]

As we go, it will be helpful to have a way to contrast a conception of kinds that takes them to be *abundant* with one that takes them to be *sparse*. The image to have is one in which there is a dense or continuous space of "plain" kinds – an abundance or plenitude of some sort – and then a different and much smaller set – a sparse set – of kinds that somehow "metaphysically stick out" or are "distinctive." I say "*metaphysically* stick out" because it the idea is that there is something distinctive about the kind itself. *Water* is distinctive in a way that *schwater* is not. Maybe that is just a matter of *water* being salient to us while *schwater* is not. But more likely, the distinctiveness of *water* is a matter of some facts about it making it metaphysically privileged – not just one more kind in the abundance.

Initially we might think of the *plain kinds* as corresponding to properties. (And at least for the initial depiction, we can think of properties as sets of objects across possible worlds.) The sparse set, the "sticking out" *kinds*, might initially be depicted as a small subset of the plain kinds.[11] In the previous example, both *water* and *schwater* are plain kinds, while *water* sticks out and *schwater* not.

The depiction in Figure 1 is very metaphorical. But the idea is that there is a dense space of properties or plain kinds, and some of them are distinctive or "stick out" in some metaphysical way. Exactly what that metaphysical way is – how to understand the third dimension in Figure 1 – will depend on the theory one has, regarding what is distinctive about *water* as compared to *schwater*.

To move to the social: social ontologists generally acknowledge that many groupings we employ in our ordinary social lives are not natural, in the sense of being independent of human interests and activities.[12] And yet, they too are sparse – the kind *restaurant* is distinctive (or "sticks out") in some sense that the kind *schrestaurant* (which corresponds to all restaurants plus all cats plus all silver salad forks) is not.

---

[10] Following Locke's distinction between real and nominal essences. See Jones 2023.
[11] This is just an initial depiction: we should not assume unquestioningly that any given sticking-out kind is identical to a plain kind.
[12] The distinction between natural and social kinds is more complicated than this: as will become clear, we will need to distinguish social factors in the *construction* (i.e., the anchoring) of a kind from social factors in the *real definition* of a kind (i.e., the characterization of the product of construction). Some kinds will be social in both senses, while others will be social on one or the other sense. But here, we are using the natural/social comparison to introduce the idea of the sparseness of social kinds.

 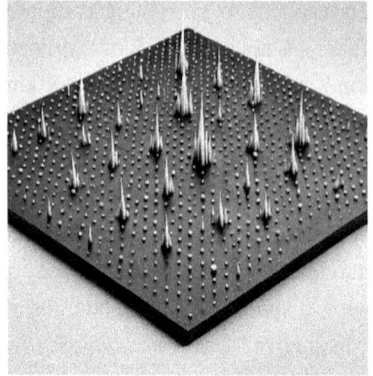

Figure 1 Space of abundant "plain" kinds vs. sparse "sticking out" kinds

As we go, I will continue to use the plain/sticking-out contrast, and I will discuss different senses of "metaphysically sticking out."[13] But I will try to be ecumenical about how it is to be interpreted. I am using the term "sticking out" exactly because it is colloquial and open to interpretation.[14]

For some theorists, the set of social kinds that "metaphysically stick out" will be *very* sparse – there is one kind *woman*, one kind *man*, one kind *marriage*, one kind *money*, and so on. Others are more pluralistic, taking there to be a cluster or range or spectrum of woman-ish kinds, man-ish kinds, marriage-ish kinds, money-ish kinds.

Similarly, theorists have different conceptions of how (or whether) kinds "metaphysically stick out." For some theorists, for a kind to "metaphysically stick out" is for it to *exist* or *be real*. Only a sparse set of natural and social kinds *exist,* while most plain kinds do not. Other theorists take social kinds to stick out only in the sense that they are named or represented, while others take social kinds to stick out only in the sense that they are salient to us. (According to these views, "metaphysically sticking out" is really a matter of contingently having a property like *being salient or being named,* rather than there being something more essential to the kind that makes it metaphysically distinctive.) Others will understand sticking out to be more or less the same as "naturalness." Others to be a matter of supporting inductive explanations. And so on.

Correspondingly, some theorists take social kinds to "stick out" in exactly the way natural kinds do. And hence take the social kinds to be a subset of the natural kinds. Others sharply distinguish social kinds from natural kinds: for a kind to be social requires that it *not* be natural.

---

[13] This is similar to the distinction Jenkins (2023) makes between "thin" and "thick" kinds. But the connotations and uses of thin and thick vary; see for instance Pagano 2023. And there is a huge literature on thick explanation (Ryle 1968; Geertz 1973; Williams 1981), which is again different.

[14] I am grateful to François Schroeter for discussion.

The Usefulness of Speaking of Social Kinds

Speaking of kinds is especially common when we are talking about *social construction*. If we are interested in the idea, for instance, that *race* is a product of social activity, it is race-kinds or racialized-kinds that we investigate. One theorist might, for instance, hold that the racialized kind *white* is constructed by group attitudes. Another by social practices. Or another by historical properties of populations.

The vagueness of the idea of a "social kind" is also in some ways an advantage: it is a bit of a placeholder for various theoretical treatments of groupings in the social world. Instead of starting with a strong theoretical commitment, we can leave it open to debate whether social kinds are universals or particulars, whether they are properties, and what roles they play in theorizing or in social life. Most importantly, we can leave it open to debate what (if anything) *metaphysically sticks out* about social kinds, as opposed to arbitrary groupings.

One difference between the way I (and the social ontology literature) will use social kinds, in contrast to some uses of kinds, is that there is typically no assumption that social kinds are essential to their members.[15] Perhaps some social kinds are, but the term is generally used more broadly than that.

I should also note that a good part of the social ontology literature speaks not of "social kinds" but of "human kinds." These are generally understood to be a subset of the social kinds. A human kind is a kind of which humans are members. So races and genders are human kinds (since individual people are the members of these kinds), while *property, restaurant*, and *dollar* are social kinds but not human kinds (since the members of these kinds are things other than people).[16]

2.2 Two Answers to "What Is X?" Questions

One way to kick off the inquiry into the nature of social kinds is to think about questions of the form "what is X?" In asking such questions, what sort of answer are we looking for?

As far back as Plato, many central philosophical inquiries take the form "What is X?": what is courage, what is justice, what is piety? These questions aim to characterize or define these categories. In contemporary philosophy, questions like these get answered by proposing necessary and sufficient conditions for being an X, or proposing analyses or definitions.

---

[15] Some kinds may be essential to their members in the sense that if an object is a member of kind X, then in all possible worlds in which it exists, it is an X.

[16] Moreover, if there are nonhuman creatures that are social, like social insects and primates, then there may be social kinds they are members of, which are not human kinds. I am grateful to Muhammad Ali Khalidi for this point and extensive comments on this section.

Alongside these inquiries – and this can be found in Plato as well – is a different set of inquiries that focus not on *defining* a kind, but on uncovering its *sources*. In *Cratylus*, for instance, Plato discusses whether words are natural, or whether they are a product of human convention. And in several dialogues (especially *Gorgias*, *Republic*, and *Laws*) the same is asked of legal categories. This is a different sort of answer to the questions "what is a word" or "what is law."

Inquiry into the sources of kinds – what makes kinds what they are – is not as prominent in contemporary analytic philosophy, but is central to other philosophical traditions. In particular, it is asked in the "social construction" tradition, especially associated with Nietzsche and Foucault. Much of this work is historical or causal, examining the social and political forces that shape the categories we possess. But questions into the sources of kind or categories are not just historical or causal: new work in social construction is making a metaphysical turn, asking how social factors metaphysically determine the existence and nature of kinds.

We thus have two facts whose determination we can talk about separately, and with them two sorts of answers to "What is X" questions: (1) What kind is X? How is X to be characterized; for instance, what plain kind does X correspond to? What ontologically determines that an object is an X? (2) What makes it the case that X is the kind it is? In virtue of what is a kind not just one among many kinds in the abundance, but instead metaphysically sticks out?

2.3 Making Sense of Social Construction

To sharpen this point – and to make some further important distinctions – it is useful to consider the notion of social construction.

The term 'social construction' has a checkered reputation. There was a time when to call something socially constructed was to commit to a particular agenda or theory about the nature of the world. It suggested the denial of realism, for instance, and to some a rejection of science. Social construction was at the heart of the culture wars in the 1980s and 1990s, so much that Ian Hacking's "The Social Construction of What?" (Hacking 1999) is largely devoted to parodying various claims of social construction.

In recent years claims of social construction have become more widespread, especially with regard to categories like race and gender, and they also have been defanged a bit, losing some of their anti-realist connotations. Which allows us to be open-minded with regard to how we should understand social construction.

Social Ontology

Social Construction as the Determination of "Metaphysical Sticking Out"

In the remainder of this subsection, I will be considering a recent prominent discussion of social construction by Sally Haslanger (Haslanger 1995). I will draw on some important distinctions she makes, but will also partly use her account as a foil, pointing out certain problems and revising them in order to propose a structure to the field.

Let me briefly preview the upshot of the next few pages. I just spoke about the idea that social kinds "metaphysically stick out," rather than just being on a par with all the miscellaneous abundance. Maybe that means that a sparse set of social kinds *exists*, or maybe it means something else. In this subsection I will argue that this is exactly the idea of social construction. To theorize about how a kind is determined to be metaphysically distinctive or "stick out" is exactly to theorize about the *construction* of the kind. Social construction is the same thing as the metaphysical determination of its sticking out. This is putting the same issue in two different ways.

This is (I contend) more accurately what people have historically been after in inquiries in social construction. In some of the literature, however, social construction is coming to be understood in a different way. And this I want to push back against, since it muddies the notion. So I want to consider Haslanger's approach, some of which I will endorse but some I will disagree with.

Haslanger's Approach to Varieties of Social Construction

Haslanger introduces a three-way distinction among different types of social construction. First is the distinction between causal (social) construction and constitutive (social) construction: the first is the claim that social factors are involved in causing a kind to be, and the second is that social factors are "constitutive" or "ontological." She then adds to this *discursive (social) construction,* according to which language or attributions are involved in construction. Here are her specific definitions, where the "somethings" she has in mind are social kinds, like gender kinds and racial kinds:

> **Causal construction:** *Something is causally constructed if and only if social factors play a causal role in bringing it into existence or, to some substantial extent, in its being the way it is.*
> **Constitutive construction:** *Something is constitutively constructed if and only if in defining it we must make reference to social factors.*
> **Discursive construction:** *Something is discursively constructed just in case it is the way it is, to some substantial extent, because of what is attributed (and/or self-attributed) to it.*

These distinctions are important. But there is something about them – especially about the definition of "constitutive construction" – that suggests they need some changes.

Reworking Haslanger's Definitions

To understand these definitions and see how they might be improved, it is helpful to clean up their structure a little (notice that "if and only if" is equivalent to "just in case"). So let us rephrase and simplify them, to bring out where they are parallel and where they are not:

> X is **causally constructed** if and only if X exists or is the way it is because (causally) of social factors.
> X is **constitutively constructed** if and only if the definition of X involves social factors.
> X is **discursively constructed** if and only if X is the way it is because (unspecified) of attributions to it.

Setting them against one another, we see some differences: both causal and discursive constructions involve some factor (the social or attribution) in X being the way it is (or existing). But constitutive construction is not put in these terms. Rather, it is put in terms of the *definition* of X. Why the change? Is the definition the thing that makes it the way it is, or do these definitions fail to be parallel?

There is also something puzzling about the causal and discursive versions. What is it to say "X is the way it is because ... "? This phrase is sort of understandable, but is also a bit hard to make sense of. If we were talking about a thing having some accidental property – like the doll having blue hair or the building being clad in brick – then we can easily see how we might give a causal explanation as to why it has that property. But here it seems we are – at least potentially – speaking of essential properties. The idea seems to be that something is causally constructed if there are social factors that causally explain its having the *definition* it does, as opposed to having some other definition. But if kinds essentially have the definitions they do, then either that just amounts to bringing it into existence or else it is nonsensical, since they *already* have the definitions they do.

Some might just assume that to construct is to-bring-into-existence: the way causal construction works is that it makes social kinds *exist*, or makes them *real*. This may be ok, but the problem is that it makes the definition of causal social construction apply only if one has some very particular ideas about social kinds and realism. However, we can weaken Haslanger's definition while preserving its spirit. That is, we can swap out the puzzling phrase about social factors making X "the way it is," and we can also take out the limitation that social kinds would not exist but for social construction.

Social Ontology

What matters is what we alluded to earlier: social construction does something to X, endows it with something, that other plain kinds lack.[17] To use that generic phrase, X somehow "sticks out," while other plain kinds do not. So a better formulation might be this:

> X is **causally socially constructed** if and only if X sticks out because (causally) of social factors.[18]

This, of course, is not particularly informative until we theorize about "sticking out." And again, different theorists can have different ideas about what sticking out amounts to. Maybe this: to *causally socially construct* a kind is to cause it to stick out in the sense that it supports inductive explanations. Maybe it is to cause it to be named or represented. Maybe it is to cause it to exist, or to be real. Maybe there are several sorts of sticking out. Part of the job of the theorist of social construction is to take a stand about this.

This, then, is a generic way of making sense of *causal social construction*, to be filled in by a substantive theory. Now let us turn to its ontological sibling.

Making the Definition of Ontological Social Construction Parallel

With this, it becomes clear why the earlier definition of "constitutive social construction" does not sit right. If causally constructing a kind causes it to be the case that the kind exists, or that it supports inductive explanations, or that it is represented, and so on, then there should be a parallel ontological version. And constitutive social construction, as characterized earlier, is not it.

Part of the problem, I surmise, is the label. When we speak of something "constituting" or "being constitutive" of something else, the constituting thing seems like it is a part of it, not a source of it. A more accurate term would be *ontological social construction*. That term, however, is awkward, and I have argued that anyway, there are also other reasons for introducing a new term. The term I like to use is "anchoring." So here is a definition:

> X is **socially anchored** (i.e., **ontologically socially constructed**) if and only if X sticks out because (ontologically) of social factors.[19]

---

[17] Again, making use of the simplification that the distinctive kinds are a subset of the plain kinds.

[18] Two comments on this. First, I have added the word "socially" into "causal construction," because it would be fine to speak of other kinds of construction, such as "causal natural construction" in which the causal factors are strictly natural. Second, we should be clear that the definition should not exclude nonsocial factors: I (and a number of other theorists) would hold that social kinds are constructed by a mix of social and nonsocial factors.

[19] In general, I use the term "socially constructed" in the ontological sense, not the causal sense. And therefore I tend use "socially anchored," "socially constructed," and "ontologically socially constructed" as synonyms.

Separate from this is the question of how X is defined. There are factors that anchor X – that is, that metaphysically make X stick out (however we interpret that). And then there is the way X is. Again the terminology is not terrific, but perhaps this will do:

> X is **socially constituted** *if and only if the real definition of X involves social factors.*

An important point to note here: it may be that whenever something is socially constructed, it is *also* socially constituted. It may even be that whenever something is socially constructed, it is socially constituted in part by exactly the factors that socially construct it. In other words, it may be that the real definition of a kind X is the *conjunction* of the anchors and the things that the anchors construct.

This is a matter of controversy. Elsewhere I have argued that "conjunctivism" is false, and that there is a sharp separation between the factors that socially construct a kind and those that compose the products of social construction.[20] Others disagree.[21] I discuss the topic a bit in Subsection 7.2, but in this Element I will remain agnostic. But in either case, it is still beneficial to separate the inquiry into *social anchors* (or *ontological social construction*) from the one into *social products* (or *the characterization,* or *real definition*). Even if the first inquiry is a piece of the second, separating them makes all the theorizing clearer.[22]

2.4 "What Is X?" and Social Construction

There are, in short, two sides of the inquiry into the nature of social kinds. One metaphysical topic in social ontology is the inquiry into social construction or anchoring. Another is the inquiry into *what* has been socially constructed, or the product.[23]

If we can make sense of *causal* social construction, it is clear that that is not an inquiry into the real definition of X. Rather, it is an inquiry into the *causal* determination of X's existing or otherwise sticking out. Similarly for *ontological* social construction. It is an inquiry into the *ontological* determination of X's existing or otherwise sticking out. There is also an ontological inquiry into the determination of that fact. Once we see that there is an ontological analogue to causal social construction, it is clear that it is distinct from – albeit complementary to – the inquiry into characterizing or defining.

---

[20] Epstein 2015, 2019a
[21] Guala 2016, Hawley 2019, Schaffer 2019, Haslanger 2016, Pagano 2023
[22] On this point, Schaffer (2019) and Jenkins (2023) have expressed agreement.
[23] Again, I will remain agnostic about whether the product – that is, what has been socially constructed – includes the anchors. I clarify this issue and discuss some implications of the alternatives in Subsection 7.2 and Section 8.

2.5 The Two-Part Inquiry in Pufendorf's Theory of Property

Recall Pufendorf's account of property from the last section, and that the first sections put forward a theory of what property "proceeds from." The key chapter in that section – chapter 4 – is called "The origin of ownership." A natural way to read that title is that the chapter is a history, an account of the causal sequence leading to the development of property. But though Pufendorf discusses the original granting of dominion over the earth to mankind by God, and though he talks about an imagined historical "community of man," the chapter has almost nothing to say about causal origins. All he says about the causal origin of property is a brief comment that forming these pacts is advantageous to mankind: "that sane reason, upon a consideration of the general state of social life, advises that this be set up and established among men" (Pufendorf IV, IV, sec. 14).

Instead, the origins he discusses are what ownership "immediately arises" from. Pufendorf does think that God is one of the sources of ownership – like his predecessors, he holds that God gives man dominion over nature. But that, he argues, is not enough: "Since all men are by nature equal, their power over creatures is likewise equal, nor with respect to creatures has one part of them been assigned to my neighbor and another to me." To produce ownership in a society, then, requires something else – tacit convention: "The only conclusion, therefore, is that the distinction between possessions is derived from a pact."[24]

Thus, Pufendorf is clear on the distinction between ontological and causal origins. The factors from which property proceeds, on his view, are tacit or explicit agreements, together with God's granting of dominion over the earth. Those are the things that stand in an ontological relation to the institution of property. Separately, there are good reasons people form such pacts. Those – together with the "general state of social life" in a particular community – are the factors that causally lead the community to form the particular pact they do. (For instance, for their pact to include a first occupancy condition on ownership.)

The benefits to mankind, together with facts about the social life of the community, are social factors that *causally socially construct* ownership. The agreements together with God's grants are the social factors that *ontologically socially construct*, or that *socially anchor*, ownership.

---

[24] Pufendorf IV, IV, sec 5. In this passage Pufendorf is describing and endorsing an argument by Velthuysen. Pufendorf goes on to apply it specifically to the basis for ownership being produced by first occupancy: "First occupancy of itself, before the existence of pacts, does not confer any right."

Pufendorf on the Products of Ontological Construction

Pufendorf's theory of the origin of ownership, then, is an ontological theory, a theory about what factors anchor ownership. But that is only the first part of his discussion of property. The more detailed discussions are the chapters we grouped into Part (II).

These chapters address which sorts of things can be owned, as well as the conditions for a property relation to hold between a person and a thing. Much of this lays out the different conditions that different societies have put in place.[25] As mentioned earlier, societies differ on their conditions for the ownership of animals, for ownership of parts of the sea, and so on. Pufendorf does not give a complete account of the conditions for ownership, largely because he cannot: it differs from society to society. But he does illustrate how such an account would go.

Diagramming the Whole Picture: Causal Construction, Ontological Construction, and Products

This brings us to a diagram we will see variations of throughout this Element. It depicts both parts of the ontological inquiry into the nature of property, adding in the causal construction for good measure.

On the left side of Figure 2 are the factors involved in socially constructing ownership. At the bottom are the causal factors, that is, the social factors which cause the ontological factors to obtain. At the top left are the ontological factors that "immediately give rise to" ownership. On the right side is the product of social construction, that is, the ownership relation, constructed as it is. And there are three arrows. Facts like the aims of the society and the benefits of property

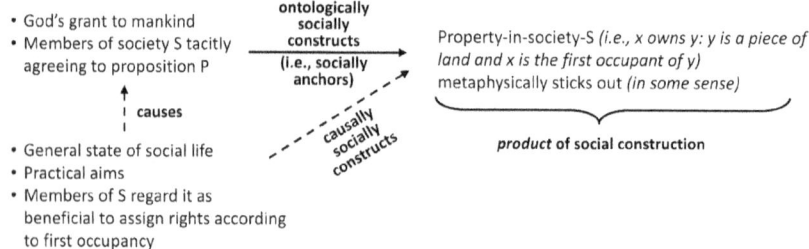

Figure 2 Components of the construction of property, using Pufendorf's account

---

[25] Pufendorf also does explain why these societies have agreed to the conditions they have. For instance, he points out that when nations started using warships, they started setting up pacts governing dominion over parts of the sea. The pacts evolve as practical uses do. Like the causal explanation of the advantages of property in general, these are causal explanations of specific conditions on ownership in a particular context.

are causes of the ontological factors,[26] and as such, they are "causal construction" factors of ownership. Facts like the tacit agreement ontologically socially construct or "socially anchor" the product.

2.6 Classifying Social Kinds

This framework helps situate and rework other proposals in the literature. For instance, Muhammad Ali Khalidi proposes a three-way division between different kinds of social kinds (Khalidi 2013),[27] which he presents in Figure 3.

The two dimensions of Figure 3 are given in the questions at the top: one is about what the *existence of the kind* depends on; the other, on what *membership in the kind* depends on. A kind like *recession*, according to Khalidi, exists even if we have no attitudes toward it. And for something to be a recession does not require that we have attitudes toward it either. For the kind *money* to exist requires that we have attitudes toward it, but particular tokens of money do not require us to have attitudes toward them. And the existence of the kind *prime minister* requires us to have attitudes toward the kind, and for something to be an instance of *prime minister* also requires us to have attitudes toward it.

We can recognize these two dimensions in the structure I have described: they are special cases of ontological social construction (i.e., anchoring) and of the conditions of the resulting kind. We can understand Khalidi to hold that

The distinction between three kinds of social kinds

	Does the existence of the kind depend on our having propositional attitudes towards it?	Does the existence of instances of the kind depend on our having propositional attitudes towards them?	Examples
First Kind of Social Kind	NO	NO	*racism, recession*
Second Kind of Social Kind	YES	NO	*war, money*
Third Kind of Social Kind	YES	YES	*permanent resident, prime minister*

Figure 3 Khalidi's classification of social kinds

---

[26] They are not the only causes: there are other causes of the community making those pacts, and of course the social factors are not causes of God's grants. It is also worth noting that there are many ways that causal construction might be social: there can be social causes of social anchors, nonsocial causes of social anchors, and social causes of nonsocial anchors. (I am grateful to Riin Koiv for this point.)

[27] See also Thomasson (2003) for a related classification.

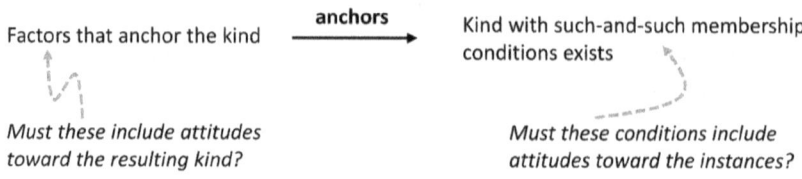

Figure 4 Khalidi's questions within our structure

the way social kinds "stick out" or are "distinctive" is *to exist*.[28] The first dimension, then, asks whether the *anchors* of a kind include attitudes toward it. The second asks whether the *membership conditions* of the resulting kind involve attitudes.

The framework, then, helps situate Khalidi's proposal (see Figure 4). But it also raises a number of ways in which Khalidi's classification can be questioned.

Khalidi classifies kinds according to whether their anchors do or do not involve attitudes toward the kinds themselves. And according to whether their membership conditions do or do not involve attitudes.

Even among these, I think Khalidi misses a category in Figure 3: namely, where the answers are NO / YES. Consider, for instance, political kinds and kinship kinds in societies that do not have attitudes toward political or kinship systems. Similarly, a participant in a gift-economy may have no attitudes toward gift-economies, yet for something to be a gift requires that the person have an attitude toward it.

But more importantly, we should observe that Figure 3 is just one of many ways of classifying kinds, and for many purposes other classifications are likely superior. We could classify kinds according with whether (or not) they are anchored by attitudes at all, not specifically attitudes that are toward the kinds themselves. Or according to whether they are anchored by *collective* attitudes – by collective attitudes that are toward the kinds themselves, and/or ones that are not. Or according to whether they are anchored by social factors that are not attitudes at all. Or whether they are partly or wholly anchored by nonsocial factors. And similarly for membership conditions. Kinds might or might not have membership conditions that include attitudes toward the kinds themselves, or collective attitudes, or social factors that are not attitudes, or that include only nonsocial factors.

---

[28] Khalidi wonders (personal communication) how it could be otherwise, since if we are doing ontology, we are surely inquiring into what *exists* in the social world. I too am inclined to favor a theory that takes social kinds like *restaurant* to exist, and *schrestaurant* not to. But there are different views, such as those that hold that *restaurant* and *schrestaurant* are ontologically on a par, with the former being distinctive only inasmuch as it is collectively represented. See Sections 5.1 and 8.1.

When thinking about classifying kinds – and about answering "what is X" questions – it is helpful to think more generally about the all the things that can go into the dimensions – that is, all the various potential factors in social construction and the various potential factors in characterizing the kind that has been constructed.

3 Two Other Cases

Social ontology is flourishing nowadays, in large part because it swims against the tides of fragmentation and specialization. So, when thinking about the field, it is productive to have a range of cases in mind. A theory that looks good for one social kind may be unworkable for another.

We also need to have a range of cases in mind if we are to understand what theorists in the field are doing, given how diverse their aims and approaches are. In this section, I introduce two other running examples in addition to property – the case of race and the case of group attitudes.

I have expressly chosen these cases to bring out contrasting features of social entities and their construction. Property is closely tied to law, though it is also economic and cultural; it is clearly a product of social structuring, at least in how it is manifested from society to society, and it typically involves relations between people and things. Races, on the other hand, are "human kinds," that is, involving the categorization of people. They have legal ramifications, but are (arguably) tied up with biological systems of classification, social and historical distributions of populations, and social and economic systems of oppression. And analyzing group attitudes – the beliefs, desires, intentions, and actions of groups of people – involves understanding whether and how groups can have cognitive properties, and perhaps even minds of their own. This is tied to questions about cognition in general, how to understand theoretical and practical activity of groups, and topics like collective responsibility.

3.1 Race and Racialized Kinds

Dominant theories of race in the eighteenth and nineteenth centuries are what we might call "old-school biological essentialism." These often involved a cluster of claims about common features – biological features and character features – possessed by members of racial groups. It is generally (although unfortunately not universally) agreed that these theories are mistaken. And not just mistaken, but also that they are tools of oppression.

It is tempting just to throw race out – to say there is not and never was such a thing as race. Some people do just that: Appiah 1985, for instance, argues that race cannot be extricated from clusters of mistaken claims, and that race is therefore an illusion.[29] There are, however, reasons to resist this move. One is that – despite confusions and even contradictions in how people apply and think about racial categories – they nonetheless use categorizations of race in many predictable ways. Another is that membership in racial categories seems to have systematic causal consequences. And another is that to abandon racial categorization may hinder efforts to remediate historical injustices.

Is there a way to make sense of race that does justice to all the complexities? The range of theories is enormous. Roughly, though, they can be split into three categories.[30] One is to reject racial categories, for Appiah's or other reasons, and to explain away their apparent applications. Second is a new naturalism – different from old-school biological essentialism, typically by stripping away the "character features" associated with racial categories and by making use of more sophisticated biological tools. In these theories race is often unpacked using contemporary approaches to population biology, such as dividing up populations of humans according to genetic patterns, ancestry, and geographic isolation. And the third category of theories is a broad one, understanding races to be "socially constituted" or "social constructs." These theories treat races as social, cultural, political, and identity categories. In all three categories of theories there is a huge variety of approaches, but the third is the most varied.

As noted earlier, races are human kinds. But interestingly, theorists are often not asking about *particular* racial categories. They are not typically asking, "what is black-in-the-contemporary-United-States?" or "what is white-in-South-Africa?" But, rather, are proposing theories in answer to the more general question, "what is race?" or "what is a race?" That is, they inquire into the nature of a kind (race) whose instances are other kinds (particular races).[31]

Therefore, many of the proposals in the literature are not of the form:

> z is a member of racial category X if and only if z is a person with such-and-such properties

But rather of the form:

> X is a race (or a racialized category) if and only if X is a kind (or category or group) with such-and-such properties.

These are related to one another, but they are not addressing the same questions. Clearly, theories of particular racial categories need to square with theories of race

---

[29] See also McPherson (2024) for a new approach to eliminating "race concepts."
[30] There are many ways theories of race have been categorized in the literature, and this is just one.
[31] Some theorists understand particular races to be groups of people; I prefer to regard them as kinds, to be more general, but the choice does not change much in understanding their nature.

in general. How a theorist analyzes a particular race needs to meet the conditions for race-kinds, and theories of race-kinds should neither over-generate nor under-generate.

Even if we focus on the latter form (i.e., the analysis of *X is a race or racialized category*), there is significant disagreement about what would count as a good answer. In Section 5, I will discuss the answers given by three different theorists – Michael Hardimon, Ron Mallon, and Katharine Jenkins – in theorizing about race. Jenkins argues that being a member of a racial category is a matter of having a certain set of constraints and entitlements. Mallon gives an account of race in which he discusses the causal mechanisms behind the characteristics and stability of racial categories. Are these views answering the same question? Are they in competition with one another?

When we set these three views against one another, it will turn out that they contribute answers mostly to distinct parts of the inquiry I was discussing in the last section. Mallon mostly talks about what I called "social construction" in the last section, and Jenkins gives an account of the product of social construction, with a general answer to the sorts of membership conditions racial categories have. It will also turn out that all three theorists roughly share a view about what makes social kinds "stick out": namely, that social kinds are kinds that support explanations or inductive inference.

The example of race, then, is a good case for examining how inquiries in social ontology can be divided, and also for using the division to clarify questions we might be interested in. The complexities associated with race also raise a range of issues that come up – or should come up – in other domains of social ontology. We have already mentioned several of these: how to deal with disagreement and uncertainty about the targets of the analysis, how to deal with interrelated hierarchies of kinds, how the inquiry can have different components or be structured. Considering race also raises questions about the existence of kinds, and the reality of social kinds; about essence and different senses of essence; about norms and their role in social kinds; about contextual restrictions to their application; and about social practices and the interaction between material facts and social ones.

And more: to what extent can we make sense of, or defend, pluralism about the nature of kinds, and to what extent is pluralism to be resisted? Especially with regard to politically important kinds, is it possible to give a purely descriptive account of their nature, or does a correct account of the ontology of kinds necessarily involve normative considerations? These are all salient to race, and plausibly to other social kinds as well.

3.2 Group Attitudes

A very different kind of case, also prominent in social ontology, is the attitudes of groups. For much of the twentieth century, it was widely regarded as an illegitimate sort of "anthropomorphizing" to ascribe agency to entities like groups, social collectives, corporations, unions, governments, and institutions. Inasmuch as it makes sense to say something like "the Supreme Court believes in the separation of powers," it was understood to be an abbreviation for the claim that all (or a majority of) the members of the Court individually have that belief. Approaches like these are sometimes called "summative" theories of group attitudes.[32]

The obvious problem with summative theories is that they are too demanding. Judges, for instance, sometimes aim to interpret a law based on the "legislative intent" of the legislators who enacted a law. But even when a majority of legislators vote for a law, it is a mistake to infer that everyone has the same intentions behind their votes. It does seem that legislature could have an intention in a "holistic" way, even if the individual legislators are at odds to some extent.

The less obvious – but more interesting – problem is that summative theories are insufficient: they are not demanding enough. Even if every legislator had the same intention – the intention to do A – there is a difference between that and for the legislature to have *that* intention. As Margaret Gilbert points out, you may intend to walk to the bank and I may intend to walk to the bank, but that falls short of *our* having the shared intention to walk to the bank.[33]

Increasingly, theorists are taking more nuanced stances. Groups, institutions, and so on do not just play crucial roles in the social world, but they seem to do so in ways that resemble how individuals do. They seem to take actions, to navigate the world in practical ways, and to bear responsibility for what they do.

There are now significant literatures on many attitudes and cognitive features of groups and other collectives, including intention, belief, acceptance, judgment, and reasoning. Typical analyses argue for conditions for a group to have a belief, often in terms of the attitudes of group members. Here, for instance, is Jennifer Lackey's characterization of group belief:

> A group, G, believes that p if and only if: (1) there is a significant percentage of G's operative members who believe that p, and (2) are such that adding together the bases of their beliefs that p yields a belief set that is not substantively incoherent. (Lackey 2021, p. 48)

---

[32] Tollefsen 2015.
[33] Important work on this topic was done by Tuomela and Miller 1988, Gilbert 1989, Gilbert 1990, Searle 1990, and Bratman 1993. Gilbert emphasizes the normative commitments we have toward one another in sharing intentions; Bratman the interlocking of our intentions to adapt to one another.

This analysis appeals to the further notions of "operative members" and the "bases of individual beliefs," in order to account for conflicts and divergences among the beliefs of the members.

Michael Bratman proposes an account of shared intention that does not aim to give necessary and sufficient conditions, but rather that offers one way that is sufficient for shared intention to arise for a certain kind of group (Bratman 1993). Bratman limits his account to what he calls "modestly social groups," which are small groups working together toward a common goal. He proposes an account for such a group to have a shared intention in terms of members of the group having intentions for the group as a whole, and also their having individual intentions to adapt their activity to contribute to the activities of others in furtherance of the goal.

Both of these accounts are "reductive," like the summative account, without regarding a group attitude A to be an aggregate of individuals having the same attitude A. Other approaches deny that individual attitudes – even structured ones, like Lackey's and Bratman's proposals – are sufficient for a group to have an attitude. Margaret Gilbert, for instance, argues that social groups have normative features that cannot be captured by individual attitudes alone, and that group attitudes involve commitments by those groups as units. Schmid (2023) argues that "plural subjects" are no less basic than individuals. Just as individual subjects have attitudes, so do plural subjects.

In some of the literature on group attitudes is there also talk of why these kinds have the characteristics they do.[34] Most common is some version of functionalism with regard to group attitudes.[35] Functionalism with regard to group attitudes is often understood to parallel functionalism with regard to individual attitudes: mental states are understood to be kinds whose members perform functional roles in cognitive systems. It is the performance of these functional roles that explain why mental states – whether they be individual or group mental states – have the characteristics they do. It is interesting to explore whether this can be understood as a theory of construction or anchoring.

Functionalism is not the only account of the sources of group attitudes. And again most theories group attitudes focus on the conditions for groups (or certain kinds of groups) to have some kind of attitudes, rather than on their sources, that is, what makes those kinds stick out. But this is one of the things that make group attitudes an interesting case for us to consider here. Examining it in tandem with the case of property and the case of racial kinds helps illustrate that – with group attitudes too – we need to inquire not just into

---

[34] We can treat them as kinds in a couple of different ways. We can rewrite them a bit (see Subsection 6.1); we can also think of tokens of group attitudes as objects.

[35] See List and Pettit 2011, Huebner 2013, Bratman 2014, Tollefsen 2015.

their membership conditions but also into what anchors them. Which in turn helps broaden our perspective on inquiries into anchoring.

3.3 Using These Cases

In the next section, I will consider a simple agreement theory for the construction of property and of race. And – though this may seem a bit peculiar – I will also consider a simple agreement theory of the construction of group attitudes. It is not that it is a good theory of any of these cases. But it helps bring out standard features of a theory of social construction, as well as requirements that such theories will need to meet.

4 Social Construction: A Simple Theory

We now have divided social ontology into two inquiries: (1) the inquiry into how the social construction of kinds works, and (2) characterizing the products, that is, the resulting kinds. And we have introduced three case studies. In Sections 4 and 5 of this Element, I focus on inquiry (1), first with a simple theory of social construction as applied to our three case studies, and then with a look at more plausible theories. In Sections 6 and 7 I turn to inquiry (2), considering simple ways to characterize social kinds (and thus to answer straightforward "what is X" questions), and then to more detailed answers.

This section, then, looks into a "toy" theory of social construction, to illustrate how we might approach theorizing about it and to draw out some requirements or desiderata for a good theory of social construction. The simple theory in this section is straightforwardly problematic. It is not absurd: to some extent it resembles theories that have been defended in the literature, and it is more reasonable than it might seem. Still, part of the aim is to see how theories can fail.

4.1 Social Construction by Unanimous Agreement

In Sections 1 and 2 I discussed Pufendorf's theory of property. In his discussion of the sources of property, he argues that it arises from tacit agreement or convention. For our purposes, I want to consider a theory that is even simpler than Pufendorf's. Namely, the theory that social kinds are products of *explicit unanimous agreement* in a community.

It is obvious that this theory cannot be correct; even 350 years ago Pufendorf found it wanting. But there are advantages to thinking through a failed toy theory. Since no one defends it, we will not need to argue whether we have set up a strawman. It *is* a strawman, yet it helps see where a theory can fail in providing either necessary or sufficient conditions for social construction.

Its clearest failure is on the necessity front. Most social kinds are not products of explicit agreement, so it could not be the full story. But that still leaves open the question of whether explicit unanimous agreement – if we could get it – would be sufficient for generating social kinds. The answer to this is less obvious, but it is likely to fail there as well.

Even a toy theory like unanimous agreement helps figure out broader desiderata for theories of social construction more generally. How can social construction possibly work: what do the anchors need to accomplish, and how can they do so? To put it in the terms we discussed in Section 2, what does a theory propose about how social kinds are distinctive or "stick out," and how does the theory take that sticking out to be determined? And what constraints are there, if any, on how social kinds can get put in place?

Finally, a toy theory also forces us to see the work required to articulate even the simplest of theories of social construction. Even this example takes some thought.

4.2 Filling Out the Details

Here is how explicit unanimous agreement might go. All the people in a community come together in some sort of meeting. Perhaps some small group drafts a proposal, or perhaps they all do it together. Then they discuss and revise it until they come to consensus. At that point, they all perform some act of agreement – perhaps they all say "aye," perhaps they raise their hands, perhaps they sign a final document – so that each member of the community individually agrees to the proposition expressed in the document. That act, according to the simple agreement theory, generates the social kind in question. (Or, perhaps more accurately, it makes it the case that the social kind sticks out in some particular way. For brevity I will speak of social construction "generating" the social kind, but as we go on, we will not be able to avoid the question of how theories differ on their views of "sticking out.")

This much describes how an agreement might be formed. But it still says nothing about what is being agreed to. To get clearer on the details of this theory, consider its application to the case of property. What might be included in the document, in order to generate a version of property? To keep it simple, let us just consider ownership of tracts of land formed by first possession, without considering other owned things, other ways of acquiring original ownership, or the transfer of ownership. So the contents of the document might be:

> *A person shall have the following rights to that land: the right to exclude others from the land, the right to enclose it, the right to use it as one wishes, and the exclusive right to the soil and plants that grow there,*

if and only if:
that person circumnavigates a tract of land up to an acre in size, and no one has circumnavigated any portion of that land previously.[36]

For convenience, let P symbolize the proposition expressed by this sentence. A simple agreement theory, then, might hold that the social kind *property* is generated by the community unanimously executing agreement to P.

4.3 Some Virtues of the Theory

Before going into the (many) problems of this simple agreement theory of social construction, we should observe that it does have some attractive features.

One nice thing is that the theory is simple enough that it is easy to express with some precision, and this helps clear up and avoid a sort of circularity that sometimes plagues theories of social construction. A different – and slightly problematic – way of putting the theory would be this: we generate the kind *property* by agreeing to the proposition *Land meeting such-and-such conditions is property*. Notice that property is what is constructed by agreement, but also is part of what is agreed to.[37] But this confusing potential circularity does not have to arise. In the way I described the theory earlier, for instance, what gets agreed to is a document, or sentence, or proposition. In agreeing to that, there is no need to have property set up in part by property itself.

Another useful feature of this theory is that it makes a clear proposal as to what the anchors of property are. According to this unanimous agreement theory, they are a collection of agreements of the form:

Person 1 agrees to proposition P.
Person 2 agrees to proposition P.
Person 3 agrees to proposition P.
Etc.

These are clear enough that we can crisply assess whether or not these agreements actually occur (or have occurred) in generating the kind *property*.

It is also somewhat clear in this theory what we take to be the *product* or *results* of the social construction. At least at first blush, what the theory claims is that the product is a social kind whose nature is that it involves certain conditions (i.e., people circumnavigating land in such-and-such a way), and that

---

[36] Formulating this in even a slightly plausible way is not as easy as one might think. I will discuss some shortcomings to this proposal later on.

[37] We can see this in Searle's discussion of how to eliminate the apparent circularity in statements of the form, "this bit of paper … is money because we believe it is money" (Searle 1998). Some implicit definitions look like this (see Gupta and Mackereth 2023), but that does not seem to be what is going on here.

attaches certain norms to things meeting those conditions. That is, the nature of the kind that is set up by agreement to P is given by the contents of P. (As I will discuss in a moment and in Section 7, things cannot be quite so clear as this.)

Finally, there is at least an intuitive sense as to what sticks out about a kind generated by unanimous agreement – and with that, an intuitive sense of *why* this sort of social construction might work. Namely, unanimous agreement seems to *bind* everyone in the community to the proposition agreed to. The theory of distinctiveness or "sticking out," then, could be that social kinds involve the community being bound to norms associated with certain conditions being fulfilled. (In this case, rights and obligations associated with a specific kind of first occupancy of land.)

All these plausible features highlight three desiderata for a theory of social construction. It is not enough for a theory just to assert that some set of anchors generates some social kind. Rather, it needs to (1) explain the connection between them, that is, why the anchors suffice for constructing that sort of kind as sticking out; (2) explain the particular sort of "sticking out" being put forward; and (3) explain why that sort of "sticking out" is the one that matters.

4.4 Flaws, At Least Some Fatal

Failures of Necessity

The most obvious flaw of this theory – as an actual theory of property – is that there never was such an agreement. I certainly have never signed such a document, and I doubt you have either. Even if the social kind *property* were formed by lawmakers or legislators (which is also probably not the case, as Pufendorf and others saw), legislation certainly does not involve unanimous agreement among members of a community.

One problem, then, is *who* needs to be involved in socially constructing a kind. A theory proposing that everyone in a community takes some action is too demanding.[38] And a second problem is what is required of the involved people. It is probably too demanding even that a significant portion take a *particular* action, or even that they have a particular attitude. At the very least, the proposal needs to be weakened: it might take fewer participants, and the demands might be less on participants.

---

[38] There is a good deal of literature in social ontology that builds from a model of consensus of some sort, in explaining social phenomena (e.g., Gilbert 2014, Bratman 2014) or consensus of a sort at least among "operative" members of a collective (Tuomela 2013). Many of us have been skeptical of this starting point (Epstein 2013, Burman 2023). See Burman for an extended critique of this sort of approach.

A different problem with the explicit agreement theory has to do with the proposition that is meant to be agreed to. Even with such a simple document as the one I described earlier, it is unlikely that people could or would be in a position to agree to it. But of course, that document is far too simple to capture the characteristics of property. It is not even clear that theorists – who work on property full time – have complete understanding of what such a proposition would contain.

So far, these are arguments against agreement of this sort occurring for actual social kinds. If we suppose that *property* is indeed an example of a social kind, that means these features cannot be *necessary* for the generation of a social kind. Unanimous agreement is too demanding for social construction.

Failures of Sufficiency

Unanimous agreement to P does accomplish *something,* with regard to the subject matter of P. It at least makes it stick out in the sense that it is unanimously agreed to. But is that the kind of metaphysical sticking-out that counts?

There have to be *some* demands on sticking-out, if social construction is not to be trivial. And remember that according to many theories, the demands are high: they hold for instance that *property* exists or is real, while *schmoperty* does not exist or is not real. Existence is nice and distinctive, as compared to nonexistence.

A reasonable guess about what a unanimous agreement theorist would regard as distinctive is this: social kinds involve being bound to certain norms, under certain conditions. That binding seemed to be a result of unanimous agreement.

One question is whether unanimous agreement actually yields the community's being bound to the norms specified in P. It is not clear it does: our simple theory has all the problems of a naïve contractualism. Suppose that our ancestors did, at some point in the past, all agree to proposition P. It is far from clear that we are bound by the rights and obligations they agreed to.

Another question is whether unanimous agreement is enough to make the kind *property* metaphysically stick out in whatever the relevant sense is. Suppose that we had made those agreements but we forgot about them, that we have no attitudes toward them today, and that we never did conduct our lives in accord with them. For *property* to be a social kind in a community at time *t* might demand that the community have certain characteristics *at t,* not just historically. Not clear that the agreements themselves do enough work.

Social Ontology 33

What Does Agreement to P Generate Anyway?

A final problem with my simple agreement theory has to do with the *product* of such a theory. That is, with the kind that supposedly gets socially constructed via everyone agreeing to P.

It *seemed* to be a virtue of the theory that the content of P – that is, the proposition that was agreed to – gives the nature of property in that society. But it is a little hard to interpret how that can be. The content of proposition P is a biconditional connecting a set of material conditions (i.e., circumnavigating a plot of land) and a set of norms (i.e., rights to use it, exclude others, etc.). What is property, then? Is property defined as that set of norms? Is it defined as those material conditions? Is it defined as the conjunction of the two? None of those seems quite right.

Moreover, it is not even clear that the nature of the product – of the constructed kind – *should* be given by the content of the proposition agreed to. Maybe agreeing to P generates a kind with conditions Q. The simple theory is, at least, incomplete with respect to what agreement generates or makes distinctive.

4.5 A Unanimous Agreement Theory Applied to Race

In the last section I divided theories of race into three categories – those that reject or radically rewrite racial categories, those that are naturalistic, and those that take race to be "socially constituted" or "socially constructed." The third category certainly should be broken down further: given the discussion in Section 2, for instance, being socially constituted may not be the same thing as being socially constructed, and different theories could be social along different lines.

But here let us explicitly consider the unanimous agreement theory as a theory of what socially constructs race. Such a theory will have analogous anchors to the ones earlier: all members of society S unanimously agreeing to some proposition, call it P_{race}.

What is the content of P_{race}? Some theorists take racial categories to have an essentially normative component – to be a member of a racial category involves having certain demands or constraints, and/or certain privileges or entitlements. If so, then P_{race} might look something like the earlier proposition involving property, with normative properties being associated with people who meet certain conditions. Other theorists take norms to accompany but not to be essential or definitional of race; instead, they take race to involve features like physical attributes, membership in ancestral groups, and geographic location. Michael Hardimon, for instance, proposes the following "minimalist" analysis of race:

A race is a group of human beings

- (C1) that, as a group, is distinguished from other groups of human beings by patterns of visible physical features,
- (C2) whose members are linked by common ancestry peculiar to members of the group, and
- (C3) that originates from a distinctive geographic location. (Hardimon 2017, p. 31)

So we could use something like this as the content of P_{race}. Now, Hardimon does not have an *agreement* theory for constructing race; rather, he finds its source in biological facts (I will discuss his view in connection with Jenkins and Mallon in the next section). Unanimous agreement is a different theory of its social construction. Still, one way a unanimous agreement theorist might go is to take the community to unanimously agree to the Hardimon version of P_{race}. Figure 5 depicts the package this theory would propose, with facts of agreement socially constructing a kind whose instances meet Hardimon's conditions.

The left side is the same as we saw for property, but with a different proposition being agreed to. The right side is the content of that proposition, along with whatever sort of sticking-out is delivered to a kind by the community unanimously agreeing to a proposition describing it.

The unanimous agreement theory is not, of course, a *good* theory of the construction of race. All of the flaws discussed with respect to property also apply to race. What I want to highlight, however, are two other interesting problems with the simple agreement theory that the case of race raises. One is the idea of agreement. It is plausible that race is not constructed by agreement, but by *conflict*: an outgrowth of difference rather than cooperative construction. And hence the case makes agreement or agreement-like theories seem naïve.

Another thing is that the unanimous agreement theory ignores *material conditions* as anchors. This is also probably a problem for property, but it is a more conspicuous shortcoming for a theory of the construction of race. An agreement theory says nothing about practices. It also says nothing about physical traits. Nor does it say anything about history, geography, or human ancestry. Nor about economics or political institutions. According to an agreement theory, the only things that figure into socially constructing the kind are the individual agreements themselves.

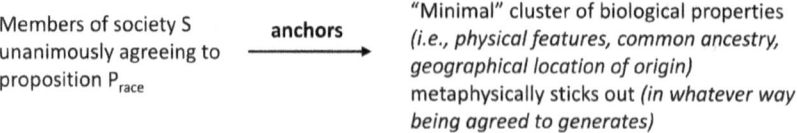

Figure 5 Unanimous agreement theory of the social construction of minimal race

The unanimous agreement theory is perhaps an extreme case, but there are many theories in social ontology that propose a very limited set of factors in social construction. My aim in this Element is not to argue for or against any particular theories. Nonetheless, it is incumbent on a theory of social construction to explain why some factors are pertinent to making kinds stick out in the sense put forward by the theory, while other factors are not.

4.6 A Unanimous Agreement Theory Applied to Group Attitudes

Now consider our third example, group attitudes. Group knowledge, for instance, or group belief, or group intention, or group preferences. The idea that these are the products of community agreement seems – and is – even more wrongheaded than the idea that race-kinds are. It is hard to believe that group attitudes are merely a matter of agreement, rather than arising from the nature of group cognition.

As mentioned in Subsection 3.2, some theories of group attitudes discuss the functional roles they play (e.g., List and Pettit 2011, Bratman 2014). This is a plausible direction for approaching the anchoring of group attitudes: if group belief, intentions, preferences, and so on do not play a reasonable role in the cognitive life of a group, then it does not matter what the community agrees to.

Still, there is a point to raising a unanimous agreement theory: one *could have* an agreement theory of the construction or anchoring of group attitudes. Just like the cases of property and race, it is sensible to inquire about the *sources* or *construction* of group attitudes. Even if a unanimous agreement theory is incorrect, it helps raise desiderata that a different theory of construction (like one along functionalist lines) ought to satisfy.

Interestingly, agreement-like theories are not quite as silly as they might seem. They might even be close to correct for related kinds. In law, for instance, it is often important to make the distinction between crimes like murder and manslaughter, trespass and burglary, false imprisonment and kidnapping. For each of these pairs, the first kind of crime involves harming others deliberately, while the second involves harming others without doing so deliberately. The term used in the law for "deliberately," which is often understood as a combination of an intention to perform the act and knowledge of the wrongness of the act, is 'scienter'. The same distinction applies in corporate law. A corporation may commit securities fraud, or it may negligently misrepresent. Here the notion is 'corporate scienter'.

Corporate scienter is clearly related to group attitudes, in particular group knowledge and group intention. It is corporations rather than groups that corporate scienter applies to, but presumably corporate attitudes are closely related to group attitudes.

Here is where an agreement theory is not so absurd: there is reason to think that the contours of corporate scienter are at least partly determined by judges for practical reasons. One problem is this: it seems to be required, for a corporation to know something, that senior officials in the corporation know it. For instance, suppose many cashiers at McDonalds know that customers are unhappy because the french fries are soggy. But suppose the higher-ups remain ignorant. Then it seems wrong to ascribe knowledge of that fact to McDonalds. The problem is that this can be (and has been) exploited to insulate corporations from being convicted of fraud. Some corporations have put systems in place to allow fraudulent activity to occur, but that screen senior officials off from knowing about that activity. Those systems block corporate scienter and hence eliminate a requirement for the corporation to have committed fraud.

Consequently, judges have changed the conditions for corporate scienter, understanding it in such a way that managers cannot intentionally insulate the corporation from liability by structuring their own ignorance of malfeasance. This, then, is a case in which the aims of judges may be partly determinative of the contours of a kind of corporate attitude.

It is still too simple to regard this as a product of agreement. Even if it is true that judges determine the contours of corporate scienter with their opinions, that is not the same thing as forming agreements. So we would still need to replace a simple agreement theory with one that takes the anchors to be – at least for some kinds – opinions issued by judges.

But though the theory is wrong, it is interestingly wrong. Not only can we can make sense of it, we can see how pragmatic considerations might lead the contours of certain corporate attitudes to be the product of practical aims, choices, and even stipulation.

5 Developing a Theory of Social Construction

In filling out the unanimous agreement theory – and seeing its shortcomings – we were able to learn something about what is required of a theory of anchoring or social construction. But it was always meant to be a toy example: some competitors are similar to unanimous agreement, but others are not. In this section I broaden our look to other ways social construction theories might go. First I roughly categorize some families of theories, to give a sense of what the landscape looks like. Then I consider the approaches of three theorists – Michael Hardimon, Katharine Jenkins, and Ron Mallon – whose theories are quite different from one another, yet all of which actually endorse a similar theory of construction. My aim, in discussing these, is to show how different actual theories can individually be understood, and also how they fit together. And from these, to distill some steps to follow in crafting any theory of social construction.

5.1 Families of Theories of Social Construction

Here – without any claim to be exhaustive – are some broad families into which theories of social construction might be categorized:

Convention-like theories. The unanimous agreement theory is a simple instance of a family of theories that take social kinds to be generated typically from structured attitudes, but sometimes certain kinds of regularities or acts, in a community. These theories include the kinds of conventions discussed by David Hume and by David Lewis, collective acceptance theories like those of John Searle and Raimo Tuomela, and perhaps H.L.A. Hart's theory of practice.

Semantic theories. A different family of theories of social construction takes social kinds to "stick out" in that (and perhaps only in that) they are represented, marked, or named. This perhaps originates with Locke's theory of "nominal kinds." The anchoring or social construction account in this model coincides with the meta-semantic account of setting up a representation or a name.

Individual mental map theories. A theory of social construction that has been widely held (especially by empiricists) is that individuals structure social kinds for themselves. According to this model, each individual person has a mental structure, web of belief, or conceptual scheme, often with associations that "carve the world" into kinds for that individual. (If these "carvings" correspond to representations, this family is close to the previous one.)

Lawmaking-like theories. These are theories that take institutions or systems to put kinds into place. They may have as inputs things like agreements, but they may also be more complex, involving things like facts of precedent, customs, and habits.

Natural-kind-like theories. Some theories regard social kinds to be constructed in a way that closely resembles a widely held view of natural kinds. That is, that social kinds stick out in the sense that they figure into explanations (lawlike or otherwise), or that they support inductive reasoning. And this is typically in virtue of some causal relations obtaining. Although it is often not explicit in these theories, some hold that kinds are anchored in a way that *guarantees* that they figure into explanations or induction, while others take a more *reliabilist* approach. That is, they hold that kinds are anchored in a way that reliably produces kinds that figure into explanations or induction. (See Subsection 5.3 for more on this.) Yet others hold there to be some measure of "naturalness" or "distance from the fundamental," where kinds (including social ones) stick out to the extent that they are natural along such a measure. For these, the theory of construction is the theory of what generates naturalness (natural laws, regularities in spacetime, etc.)

Functionalist theories. There are a great many ways functions can figure into social kinds, and many theories involving functions are really theories of the *products* of social construction rather than of social construction itself (see Subsection 7.1). But there are also theories that take functions – in some way or other – to generate kinds. Functionalist theories in sociology (like the work of Bronisław Malinowski and Talcott Parsons) tend to be theories of *causal* social construction, but there may be varieties of ontological construction that are analogous. In Section 3, for instance, I mentioned functionalist theories of mental states, which arguably involve an ontological connection between the functional roles and the characteristics of kinds of mental states.[39]

Material-basis theories. A large, but inchoate, class of theories takes social kinds to be generated from patterns in material practices, economics, technology, and the built environment. These might include theories of practice and economic or technological substructure theories. With these theories, it can be difficult to disaggregate causal from ontological construction.

This list is far from exhaustive, and the families are vague. It is also possible that these families overlap: it could be, for instance, that the way to reliably generate explanatory kinds is via convention, or naming, or lawmaking. Nor is it obvious that we should choose just one: I personally have argued for pluralism about the mechanisms of social construction.[40]

But this categorization does at least dip our toes in the water. The unanimous agreement theory was useful as a first illustration of how a theory of construction might be put together; with these, similar illustrations could be developed for other alternatives.

5.2 Reading Theories in the Literature

I now turn to proposals by Hardimon, Jenkins, and Mallon, regarding race. Their theories are very different from one another: Hardimon argues for a biologically real "minimalist" theory of race. Jenkins argues for a social constructionist theory of race in which races are clusters of "constraints and entitlements." And Mallon argues for a constructionist theory that takes races to be "homeostatic property clusters." Yet they have more in common than it might seem. All three take a similar approach to social construction: they all endorse

---

[39] Much of the literature on these theories has turned on the distinction between "role-kinds" and "realizer-kinds." This distinction has always been fraught; it may be that new thinking about ontological sources can cut some of these knots.

[40] Epstein 2014.

Social Ontology

versions of the natural-kind-like approach. By considering them all together, we can see how we might understand theories in the literature and also bring out some features and desiderata of theories of social construction.

In the last section, I mentioned Hardimon's minimalist analysis of race, in which race is analyzed in terms of three conditions on groups of humans – patterns of physical features, common ancestry, and a distinctive geography. Hardimon argues that minimalist race is a biological category:

> Minimalist race is biologically significant by virtue of being defined in terms of a biological trait that has medical and ecological significance ... Being relevant to general explanatory aims of biology ... it counts as a biological kind as well. The fact that minimalist race is a legitimate biological kind is a reason to regard it as biologically real. (Hardimon 2017, p. 81)

Race, according to Hardimon, is biologically real in virtue of two things: (1) being defined in terms of biological traits, and (2) those traits being of biological significance. In other words – to use the distinction from the last several sections – we can understand Hardimon as arguing that minimal race is biologically *constructed* and also biologically *defined*.[41] Figure 6 depicts these components of Hardimon's proposal.

On the left side of the diagram are the anchors, or the facts about the world that "construct" the kind. Notice that in Hardimon's account, the factors are not social (as was depicted in Figure 5), but biological.[42] (Although I will not discuss it much in this Element, we can talk about anchoring or construction as a product of nonsocial factors, just as we can of social factors. See Subsections 2.3 and 2.6 for a brief discussion.) Actual biological patterns make it the case that certain particular minimal clusters of biological properties are explanatory.[43] And for Hardimon, to be biologically explanatory amounts to being biologically real.

In some ways, Jenkins' theory of race could not be more different. Jenkins (2023) proposes that race is socially constructed, and that there are three sorts of

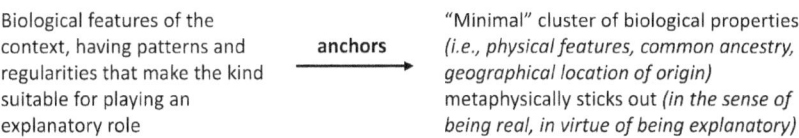

Figure 6 Hardimon's theory of minimal race as biologically real

---

[41] That is, the real definition of the kind involves only categories that would be used in biological theorizing. It is a burden on the theorist to pin down exactly what these are.
[42] Cf. Hardimon 2017, pp. 80–82.
[43] I say "actual" because it is not clear how the account is to go in counterfactual cases.

racial kinds: hegemonic, interpersonal, and identity. What defines a racial kind, for Jenkins, is a set of enablements and constraints. Among the constraints associated with a particular racial kind, for instance, may interpersonal constraints, involving limitations to people's actions based on actions by others, environmental constraints, involving limitations based on material facts about the environment, and more. Each racial kind, then, is associated with different clusters of enablements and constraints.

But interestingly Jenkins, like Hardimon, argues for the natural-kind-like approach to social construction. She is more ecumenical about the sort of explanation that works, but nonetheless holds that social kinds are real inasmuch as they are explanatory: "I take social kinds to be a particular variety of explanatory kinds, which is to say, kinds – groupings of things in the world – that can figure in successful explanations."[44] For Jenkins, it is social – and in particular emancipatory – explanatory projects that racial kinds figure into. And the patterns that anchor racial kinds (i.e., that generate the clusters of constraints and enablements) are, for Jenkins, not strictly biological. Rather they are patterns of psychology, action, and material conditions.[45] Still, for Jenkins – just as for Hardimon – racial kinds stick out in being explanatory, and their explanatoriness is constructed by patterns that make them suitable for playing an explanatory role. I depict it in Figure 7, putting in bold what Jenkins shares with Hardimon.

The sorts of anchors are different, and the resulting kind is different. But their approaches to construction are, if not the same, at least in the same family.

Turning to Mallon's account, it appears quite different from both Hardimon's and Jenkins'. Yet he too puts forward a natural-kind-like theory of social construction.

Mallon 2016 proposes a theory of the construction of human kinds (with racial kinds as the paradigmatic example) that draws on the idea of a "homeostatic property cluster" from the literature on natural kinds.[46] His account aims to

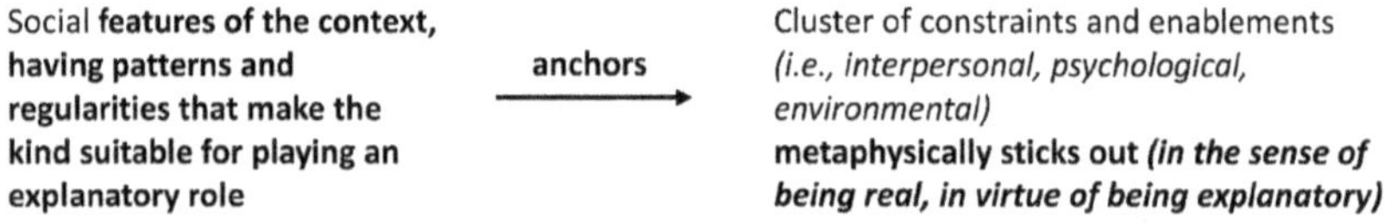

Social **features of the context, having patterns and regularities that make the kind suitable for playing an explanatory role**   *anchors* ⟶   Cluster of constraints and enablements *(i.e., interpersonal, psychological, environmental)* **metaphysically sticks out** *(in the sense of being real, in virtue of being explanatory)*

Figure 7 Jenkins' theory of the construction of racial categories

---

[44] Jenkins 2023, p. 78   [45] See Jenkins 2023, pp. 183–88, for discussion of this breakdown.
[46] That is, clusters of properties that are co-instantiated over time due to a homeostatic causal mechanism; see Boyd 1999.

describe mechanisms that stabilize certain ways of classifying and treating people. There are two components to Mallon's story: (1) there are social roles that people are put into, the roles playing a part in certain social mechanisms; and (2) people come to represent those roles and share knowledge of those representations. These two components interact causally with one another: the roles and mechanisms affect the representations, and the representations affect the roles. It is possible for such causal systems to be entirely unstable, but often they reinforce one another in a stable way. For these, we can be representing a stable kind that plays a role in inductive reasoning.

Mallon is not a fan of the distinction between causal and ontological construction. Still, I think it is reasonably accurate to depict his theory in the following way.[47]

In Figure 8, the dotted arrows represent causal influence or determination, and the solid arrows represent ontological operations or relations. Most of the action in his theory takes place in the causal structures that give rise to stable patterns. At the bottom left of the diagram is the system of social roles and people's representations that causally interact with one another to make a cluster of properties involved in a stable pattern. That cluster thereby becomes causally significant, which for Mallon is the sort of sticking-out that real kinds have.

Thus Mallon takes racial kinds to be anchored much as Hardimon and Jenkins do. He disagrees with Hardimon on what generates the patterns, and unlike Jenkins, he focuses on the social factors generating the stable patterns rather than the characteristics of the kinds that result from them. But for all of them, the anchoring (or ontological construction) fits the same model: it is patterns or regularities underwriting their success in explanation that make racial kinds stick out or be real.

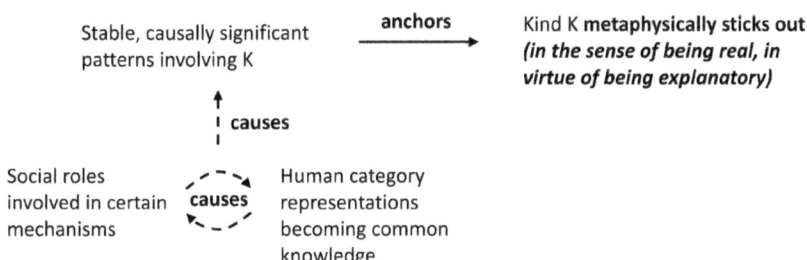

Figure 8 Mallon's model for the social construction of human kinds

---

[47] A full account would require discussion of various interpretations of homeostatic property cluster theories and their metaphysics, which would be a distraction here.

Seeing the Structure in the Theories

Hardimon gives a theory both of the anchors and of the definition of the kind. He also gives a brief account of the biological factors that anchor the fact that the kind is explanatory.

Jenkins' focus is on the right side of the diagram. She argues that there are three different kinds of kinds, each of which is characterized by different clusters of constraints and enablements. She argues that these are explanatory, in virtue of practices, but otherwise says little about the left-hand side.[48]

For his part, Mallon focuses on the left-hand side and says little about the right-hand side. The theory argues for mechanisms that generate a kind of stable equilibrium, which results in clusters of properties standing in causally significant patterns.

Hardimon's theory is clearly at odds with the two others. Both Jenkins and Mallon reject a biological account of the anchors of racial kinds. Jenkins also explicitly rejects a biological definition of racial kinds, while Mallon probably would also reject it. Meanwhile, there is some likelihood that Mallon's and Jenkins' theories are somewhat complementary: they are mostly concerned with different topics.

How do we assess theories like these, and more importantly, how do we build a satisfactory theory of social construction ourselves?

5.3 Building a Theory of Social Construction

Setting these theories against one another – and against the unanimous agreement theory we discussed in Section 4 – helps us see not only what they are aiming at and how they fit together, but also where they need to be filled out if they are to be satisfactory theories of social construction.

The way to think about building a theory of social construction, I propose, is to begin with some assumptions and then to revise and edit repeatedly. We need to start with assumptions because there are so many variables or moving parts, in a complete theory of social kinds. Namely, there are:

(1) various ways to understand the kinds that get constructed;
(2) various ways to understand sticking out;
(3) various ways to think about how the work of social construction gets done, and
(4) various ways to think about the "inputs" to social construction.

---

[48] Interestingly, it seems that distinguishing at least some of the three categories of kinds Jenkins discusses arguably should involve distinguishing different sorts of anchors. In particular it seems that a hegemonic kind is hegemonic not only in having constraints and enablements involving domination, but in being socially constructed by certain kinds of social structures. See Jenkins 2023, p. 120.

If the aim is to focus on theories of social construction, one strategy is to start with assumptions on the right-hand side of the diagram – that is, regarding the constructed kinds and metaphysically sticking out – and then to develop theories about how those products get constructed. One should do this with the understanding that those assumptions may have to be revised, and the whole process repeatedly iterated.

For instance, one might start with a theory like Jenkins' regarding social kinds being bundles of constraints and enablements, and sticking out in the sense that they serve in emancipatory explanations. And then we can develop a theory of construction meant to account for how those get constructed. But it may be that kinds-as-constraints-and-enablements does not really square with the idea that they are explanatory kinds. Or it may be that the theory holds together better if we constrain the anchors in some way, which in turn affects how we understand the resulting kinds. In developing a theory, it is incumbent on us to ensure that the parts harmonize with one another.

If we do – at least provisionally – plant a stake in the ground regarding the resulting kinds and how they stick out, then we have some clear demands on the theory of social construction for generating them. In particular:

What does the theory of social construction aim to account for? How general is it? A theory might propose to account for the social construction of a particular kind, like property (e.g., Pufendorf). Or it might propose to account for the construction of a class of kinds, like racial kinds (e.g., Hardimon). Or of a broader class, like human kinds (e.g., Mallon). Or it might propose to account for the construction of social kinds in general (e.g., Searle). For any of these, the theory needs to be clear on whether it is accounting for how kinds are actually anchored, or giving sufficient conditions, or giving necessary conditions, for the target class.

Does the theory provide a full account of the anchors? A theory of social construction needs to be clear on the specific factors – or, if it is a more generic theory, the sorts or classes of factors – that do the work of ontological social construction. The unanimous agreement theory was relatively straightforward on this front: it was the individual agreements to a particular proposition. For the natural-kind-like theories, the anchors seem to be regularities or patterns in the actual world, though it is not always clear which ones are the pertinent ones.

What does the work of social construction? Candidates include: particular facts and events in the world; patterns in the world; individual attitudes or representations; practices; individual actions; diachronic facts. One way to work this out is by thinking counterfactually: if one of these candidates were changed, would the kind still get anchored?

Another question is whether social construction is mediated by way of a *process* or *schema*. For instance, earlier I mentioned taking a *reliabilist* natural-kind-like approach to social construction. We might not require of a particular that it actually figures in inductive explanations; but instead, that the way it is anchored reliably anchors kinds that do figure into inductive explanations. (This is a variety of natural-kind-like construction that is not discussed much in the literature, but that perhaps should be. It is plausible, for instance, that some chemical kinds are chemical kinds because they fit a pattern, not because they individually serve in inductive explanations. For instance, consider a chemical structure whose instances are, for some reason, very short-lived and oddly behaved. So they never figure in robust causal relations. That structure still plausibly qualifies as a chemical kind, because chemical structures like it reliably serve in inductive explanations, even if that one does not.) A theory may then want to characterize the anchors as sets of inputs and processes, rather than just as inputs.

The more general point is this: if one does not have an explicit account of the things that are doing the construction work, one does not really have a theory of social construction.

Does the theory account for the characteristics of the resulting kind, and for how that kind comes to metaphysically stick out in the assumed sense? Recall that we are starting with a fixed view on the product of social construction: how to understand the sticking-out of social kinds, and what the characteristics of the resulting kinds are. The demand, then, is for the theory of social construction to explain how the anchors generate those results.

There are two crucial components of this demand. One is to explain what is it about the anchors that generate the proposed sort of sticking out. For example, if sticking-out is interpreted as existence, how does the obtaining of the anchors make it the case that a kind exists? If sticking-out is interpreted as involving binding norms, or as being named or represented, or as supporting inductive explanation, how does the obtaining of the anchors make those obtain?

Second – and this is a detailed and complicated demand – what is it about the anchors that make the kind (or class of kinds) have the features that it does (or that they do)? How do the anchors specified in answer to the preceding question yield this specific kind – this kind with the characteristics it has, corresponding to one particular plain kind out of the plenum of plain kinds – to stick out in particular?

How does the theory relate to alternatives? How does it fit into a metatheory – that is, a theory of theories – of social construction? According to many theorists, the proposals regarding the construction of kinds are universal or unique. Those who take a natural-kind-like approach often argue that the nature of kinds *in general* is that they support inductive explanation (or something similar). John Searle argues that "***all*** *of human institutional reality is* created and maintained in existence by (representations that have the same logical form as) status function declarations" (Searle 2010, p. 13 [bold added for emphasis]). Given a particular theory of social construction, is it being put forward as the *only* way of anchoring or constructing this particular fact? Of anchoring social facts in general? A theory of social construction needs to be clear on its theoretical aims: to show the actual way some or all kinds are construction, to show how actual kinds could have been constructed, to show how possible kinds could be constructed, and so on.

A unitary theory of social construction needs to account not just for why its way is sufficient for anchoring social kinds (i.e., for making them stick out in the relevant way), but why it is necessary. (And equally, why the notion of sticking out it employs is the only one.) A pluralist theory of social construction does not need to argue that any one sort of social construction is necessary. But it does need to account for how a range of varieties of social construction can each be sufficient. And perhaps it needs to account for how, taken all together, they are exhaustive.

It may seem odd to ask for a meta-theory at all. One might think that that is the job of a theory of social construction: if you need to justify it with a meta-theory, you are not really giving a full theory. The problem is really that extant theories do not often rise to this task. They propose an approach to social construction without forthrightly considering whether there could be other avenues to arrive at the products they take social construction to generate. And, if not, why not?

6 Characterizing Social Kinds: Starting Simple

So far I have largely focused on how to develop a theory of social construction, or the left-hand side of the diagrams from the last couple of sections (see Figure 9). In this section and the next I turn to the right-hand side.

At various points I have said that the right-hand side of the diagram depicts the *products* of social construction, the *kinds* that get constructed, or the fact that certain *kinds stick out* in some particular way. I have also said that the right-hand side depicts one sort of answer – the most common sort of answer – to a "what is X" question. Namely, the answer that *characterizes* X, often in the form:

   z is X if and only if ... *z* ...

How are these all the same thing?

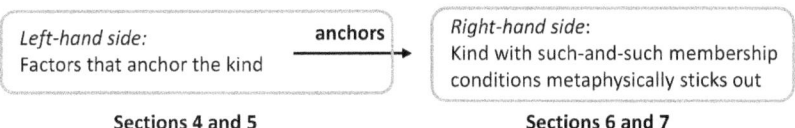

Figure 9 Section topics

As we discussed in Section 2, a simple way to think about it is to distinguish plain kinds (which are abundant) from sticking-out kinds (which are sparse). What social construction does, on this picture, is to make it the case that some plain kind has the property of sticking out, or else to create a sticking-out kind that *corresponds to* some plain kind. Thus, in answer to a question, "what has gotten socially constructed," it is correct to say that some kind (property, race, collective belief, etc.) has been made to stick out. But a more informative answer is to say *which* plain kind has been made to stick out (or which one is the correlate of the newly constructed kind). And that is what is given with *z is X if and only if . . . z . . . .*

Filling out a biconditional like this this is what many – I would venture to say most – theories in social ontology aim to do. It is a high bar, and many theories aim to do less. But it is also arguable that we should aim to do more. As I have discussed, other aims of social ontology are to give accounts of social construction (not just characterizing the products) and also to theorize about sticking out. Even characterizing social kinds, though, might involve more than an *if and only if*. After all, the simple model of plain kinds and sticking-out kinds – especially where plain kinds are identified with properties and properties with extensions across possible worlds – is not the only model we might use.

To examine, fill out, and perhaps challenge the *if and only if* (i.e., biconditional) formulation for characterizing social kinds, there are two things to consider: (a) what it is that a theory of the product is supposed to give us, for example, biconditionals, or real definitions, or essences, or otherwise; and (b) what sorts of conditions get filled in for the ellipses in " . . . *z* . . . "

In this section I will start with a simple theory, as I did for the discussion of social construction. Here the theory is "psychologism," that is, the view that – for social kinds – the ellipses should get filled in with psychological properties of individual people.[49] And, in this section, I will stick with analyses in the form of biconditionals. I will consider virtues and flaws with this theory, as it gets applied to group attitudes, racial kinds, and property. This again gives us a baseline against which to consider alternative approaches to both (a) and (b) in Section 7.

6.1 Characterizing Group Attitudes

In discussing group attitudes earlier, I was placing them into a bit of an unusual context. I was discussing approaches to the ontological construction or anchoring of kinds, and suggested that group attitudes may need such an account, just as kinds like property and race do.

---

[49] Psychologism is a very strong variety of "ontological individualism," as discussed in the philosophy of social science. See Epstein 2015, chapter 1.

Most work on group attitudes, however, focuses on the right-hand-side of the diagram, that is, on the conditions for a group to have an attitude of some kind. In Section 3, I mentioned Jennifer Lackey's characterization of group belief:

> A group, G, believes that p if and only if: (1) there is a significant percentage of G's operative members who believe that p, and (2) are such that adding together the bases of their beliefs that p yields a belief set that is not substantively incoherent. (Lackey 2021, p. 48)

I bring it up again because this proposal has a standard and familiar form, and it is worth observing some characteristics. The first observation is about the content of the analysis. What is being analyzed is a kind of attitude possessed by a group, and the analysis is given entirely in terms of the attitudes of group members. In this sense, then, it is an instance of a psychologistic analysis.

Second – and this point is rather obvious but still worth pointing out – the analysis is an abbreviation. The idea of giving an analysis with a biconditional is to give the *membership conditions* or *instantiation conditions* for the thing being analyzed. An analysis of the form

(1) z is X if and only if . . . z . . .

aims to give the conditions for anything such that if it satisfies those conditions, it is a member of that kind, and if it fails to satisfy those conditions, it is not a member.

But, of course, this form makes no sense unless there is an implicit assumption about what can be substituted for z. Often, the way this is fixed is by quantifying over a restricted domain, as Lackey does, with something like:

(2) For any group G and proposition p, G believes that p if and only if . . . G . . . p . . .

Even with this, it is still an abbreviation. An analysis like this is generally understood to have modal force: it is not just analyzing actual groups and the propositions they believe, but to give the conditions for what they might believe, or what they would have believed if the circumstances had been different, or what possible groups would believe. The simplest way to understand the implicit modal force of such an analysis is to take it to hold necessarily:

(2*) Necessarily, for any group G and proposition p, G believes that p if and only if . . . G . . . p . . .

It is not obvious (2*) is a correct interpretation: it may be that it only is meant to apply to a limited range of possibilities or contexts. If so, we do not really have a complete analysis until we resolve how broadly it is meant to apply.

Third, the form of this analysis is a little different from the standard form I have been using. I have been talking about social kinds and the analysis of their membership conditions, with formulas like (1), which unabbreviated is:

(1*) Necessarily, for all z, z is X if and only if . . . z . . .

And formulas (2*) and (1*) are a bit different from one another. It is worth noticing this, and also seeing that it can be useful to transform (2*) into something closer to (1*). One problem with (2*) is that it is not altogether clear which kind is being analyzed. Is it *belief*, as applied to a specific domain of belief-holders? Or is it *group belief*, which may have very different conditions from belief? And another problem is that (2*) pulls the domain restrictions outside of the analysis. This seems innocuous, but it can be misleading.

If we take ourselves to be analyzing *group belief*, the members of which are group-proposition pairs, then we can recast the formula as:

(2**) Necessarily, for all z,y, group-believes(z,y) if and only if z is a group, y is a proposition, and . . . z . . . y . . .

This may seem only to complicate what seemed like a clear formulation in the first place. But when we do this – and especially when we put all the givens and the domain restrictions into the analysis – we are forced to be clear about what the kind applies to and what it does not.

It also forces us to be clear about restrictions to specific times and to specific contexts. Many controversies in social ontology turn on when a person comes to have, or ceases to have a social property, depending on what is going on at that time or depending on what context that person is in (see Subsection 7.2). These can get confused if it is not clear how membership conditions involve times and contexts.

Putting everything in explicitly can make the analysis clunky. But a good strategy is to start with the clunkiest and most precise specification, to keep from overlooking crucial components. Important questions about social kinds, such as whether they can "travel" (i.e., apply in contexts other than the one in which they are constructed),[50] turn on exactly which contextual factors are included in a kind's membership conditions. It is impossible to treat this clearly without being explicit about where contextual factors fit in the analysis.

Finally, a formulation like (2**) forces us to clarify exactly how much in the analysis of a social kind we take to be a matter of individuals' psychological or mental states. In some social ontology literature, it is argued that membership in social kinds can only be – must be – a matter of the attitudes people take toward one another and things. On this view, to be a member of a social kind is to be

---

[50] See Mallon 2004 and Subsection 7.2.

thought of in a certain way. We can see this in popular theories about kinds like money, where it is seen to be only a matter of people believing that it is valuable, with the corresponding idea that if those beliefs were to go away, the kind would collapse like a house of cards. (It is sometimes unclear whether such theorists are psychologistic about the *anchors* of kinds or about the *membership conditions*.) When we insist on a complete and explicit analysis of the kind, we see what it would take to give fully psychologistic analyses of all the components. This can be a problem for conditions like *being a group* or *being a corporation* – the sorts of things to which we often ascribe group attitudes.

In this subsection I have used group attitudes to (a) clarify some aspects of the biconditional form for characterizing kinds, and (b) illustrate a psychologistic approach to the content of this characterization. In the next two subsections I consider psychologistic analyses of race and property. Again, that is not to endorse such analyses, but to illustrate how one might theorize about the right-hand side.

6.2 Psychologism and Characterizing Race

Ásta's "conferralist" theory (Ásta 2018) is a recent and bold proposal that argues for a kind of psychologism especially regarding kinds like gender-kinds and racial-kinds.

Ásta's theory is best understood as a theory of the membership-conditions of social kinds, rather than of the anchoring or construction of kinds. She argues that social kinds are much like strikes in baseball, where what makes something a strike is that an umpire confers that status on an event. Where a strike is conferred by a single individual, kinds like racial kinds are conferred, according to Ásta, by groups of people in contexts. On Ásta's view, these conferrals can change from context to context. So the conditions for being a member of a racial kind involve having a particular status conferred on a person within a local context.

To clarify her view, Ásta uses Khalidi's classification of kinds that I discussed in Section 2. Ásta argues that social kinds – and in particular gender and racial kinds – fit into Khalidi's third category of kinds. That is, their existence depends our having propositional attitudes toward them and the instances also depend on our having propositional attitudes toward them. In fact, Ásta's view is stronger than that. Not only does membership in a gender or racial kind depend on attitudes, but it is determined by nothing but attitudes. That is, by conferrals. Ásta puts forward this general formula:

> *S's judgment that X meets conditions K in C confers being B onto X. (Ásta 2018, p. 27)*

That is to say: the thing that confers being B – for example, being a member of a given racial kind – is the judgment of people (S) in the relevant context (C) that a person X satisfies conditions K. It is not the fact that X *does* satisfy conditions K, that makes S a member of B. On Ásta's account, it is the judgment – and judgment alone – of the relevant people. Nonpsychological features, like bodily characteristics or ancestry, do play a kind of role in Ásta's account. But they are not among the conditions for a person's being a member of a racial kind. It is the fact that the conferrers *take* a person to have those characteristics – whether they have them or not – that confers a racial status on the person.

The conferrals in Ásta's account, then, only involve psychological states of people. It also is clear, in this account, how membership in a racial kind depends on context. In contexts in which these judgments are made, the person is a member; where they are not, the person is not.[51] With the caveat that Ásta does not specify the modal scope of her account (so the following might need to be modified), her analysis can be cast in a fully explicit form:

> *Necessarily, for all z, c, z is white if and only if (and because) z is a person and c is a context and z is in c and the people S in c judge that z meets conditions K_{white}.*[52]

Many theories of race take an opposing position, with membership in a racial category involving material or physical conditions. To contrast Ásta's view with Mallon's, for instance, Mallon could agree that social practices and representations figure into the ontology of racial categories, but those would be part of the social construction of race. For Mallon, practices and representations generate a distinctive cluster of properties, and at least part of what it is to be a member of a racial category is to have these properties. Which could include physical properties, ancestral properties, and so on.

6.3 Psychologism and Characterizing Property

It is also possible, I suppose, to take a psychological view of property, as with the other cases. The analysis might look something like this:

> *z owns y if and only if everyone in the community believes that z is the first occupant of y and that there was no previous occupant.*[53]

---

[51] This aspect of the view is the basis for a number of critiques of Ásta's theory, since it makes membership in gender and racial kinds more ephemeral than many argue it should. See for instance Roth (2023).

[52] Even here, there are the conditions *being a person* and *being a context*, which are presumably not psychological properties. So it is nuanced how exactly to understand 'psychologistic'. I am also grateful to an anonymous referee for pointing out that Ásta's analysis should be characterized as involving a "because," rather than just being cashed out in modal terms. See Subsection 7.3.

[53] Here I am not following my own insistence on explicitly including all the quantifiers and restrictions in the analysis. I do that in the interest of readability, but am dismayed by my own hypocrisy.

This would not be a first-occupant theory of ownership, but a believed-to-be-first-occupant theory. Some theorists of social kinds find this kind of approach appealing, often with the argument that social properties can only matter inasmuch as they affect our thinking, and hence our behavior. So whenever there is a gap between the material conditions and our beliefs about those conditions – like a piece of property that was first occupied by someone but no one believes it – that gap is inert. It only makes sense, on such a view, for the psychological or epistemological features to figure into membership of the social kind.[54]

6.4 Takeaways from Simple Characterizations

The aim of this section was not to argue for or against any of these characterizations, but to fill out some illustrations. The form of all these characterizations has been a necessitated and universalized biconditional, giving the membership conditions for the kind: *Necessarily, for all z, z is X if and only if ... z ....* In discussing these biconditionals, I argued for the virtues of placing all the constraints and restrictions within the " ... z ... " portion of the analysis, rather than pulling them out up front. Otherwise we do not really get an account of all the conditions for something to be an X. Once we start allowing ourselves to pull restrictions out of the analysis, there is nothing to stop us from pulling any conditions we want out front. Which means that covert work is done by the domain restrictions, which we do not see in the analysis itself. Moreover, if we restrict the domain of the analysis, it can be unclear how (or if) the kind applies to things outside of that domain. All this militates for an explicit analysis of the complete membership conditions for the kind.

In this section I have also considered characterizations of social kinds that have a specific sort of *content*. Namely, those that take membership conditions to be a matter of the psychological states of people. My aim has not been to argue for or against psychological conditions, but to show how one might fill out such an analysis, and to raise a few of the difficulties such an analysis might face.

7 Ways to Characterize Social Kinds

Both aspects of the characterization of kinds discussed in the last section – the biconditional formulation and the psychologism – can be challenged. In this section I explore alternative approaches to the *content* of a characterization of a kind, as well as alternatives to the *biconditional form*.

---

[54] See Guala (2022) for a nuanced argument along these lines.

The first and most obvious change is to drop the limit to psychological properties. What else can figure into the conditions, and what else ought to be included in an analysis of social kinds? This is a big topic, so I focus on four: functions, material conditions, norms, and context.

Then I turn to alternatives to biconditionals. Some theories aim to provide *less* than a biconditional: they aim to give a partial nature of a kind or a class of kinds. Among these are theories that propose sufficient but not necessary conditions, and theories that propose necessary but not sufficient conditions.

More recently, a number of theorists have argued that necessitated and universalized biconditionals – despite how challenging it already is to come up with them – is still not quite enough. Many of these considerations arise from the "post-modal" revolution in metaphysics that has been going on in the last decade or two. What we need instead, these theorists hold, is an account that provides more than a biconditional. The most widely discussed involve notions such as *grounding*, *essence*, and *real definition*. I go on to consider other ways that even these post-modal considerations may not be enough, and that a full characterization of a kind may need still more.

7.1 The Sorts of Factors in the Characterization

In Section 6 I considered purely psychologistic conditions. A different answer is that anything goes: any kind of property or condition can show up in the analysans. While my own view is that "anything goes" is roughly correct, it is not particularly informative. For many social kinds, there is interesting structure to their membership conditions. In this subsection, I highlight a few candidates.

Functions

Many analyses of social kinds argue that they involve functions – in one way or another – in their membership conditions. The most straightforward way is for functions to be understood as *causal roles,* and for it to be a requirement for members of a kind to play the role.

For instance, ownership might require that the owned object plays a particular role in the practices of the community. So an analysis of ownership might be something like:

> z owns y at t if and only if y is treated by z in certain ways at t and people in z's community treat y in certain ways with respect to z at t.

A thing is owned by a person, that is, exactly when the person and the thing are playing their respective roles. Now, this is not the most plausible treatment of ownership, since it implies that the moment something ceases to be treated in the appropriate way, it is not owned; and if the treatment restarts, it becomes owned again. The literature on functions has long recognized that we need to make sense of *mal*functioning. Simple causal role functions do not allow this: if being a member of a kind X is a matter of playing a causal role, then something failing to play that causal role simply fails to be a member.

Since the 1980s an enormous literature has grown on functional kinds, largely from philosophy of biology. Ruth Millikan's theory of "Proper function," for instance, holds that something is a member of a kind just in case it is a member of a family of things that are reproduced or copied, and having the reproduced or copied characteristics they do because having those characteristics normally allows them to perform a functional role.[55] Rob Cummins also has a widely discussed approach in which things have functions in virtue of performing roles in systems that are part of larger systems.[56] Both of these (and the many variants descending from them) are ways functions might be incorporated into the membership conditions of kinds.

Another role for functions arises in theories that take social entities to be artifacts, and social kinds to be artifactual-kinds. On this topic too there is a large literature;[57] the simplest idea is something like: *z is an artifact if and only if z was created with the intention that it play such-and-such a causal role.* Here, the actual performance of the causal role function is not the condition on z to be an artifact; the condition is the intention. A standard example of an artifactual kind is a hammer. Something is a hammer, on this theory, just in case it was created with the intention that it perform the function of knocking in nails. So the function is part of the analysis of the kind, but it is not the performance of the role itself that is a condition for z to be a hammer; rather, it is that z bear a relation to a person and to that person's attitude toward a function – namely, that z be created by the person and that the attitude be a cause of the person's creating z.

Many of the ways we think about kinds as functional do *not* involve functions in the membership conditions of kinds. But instead, as functions figuring into in the social construction of the kind – sometimes the causal social construction, sometimes the anchoring. Much of the discussion of the functions of social kinds is not, therefore, a topic for this section, but rather is about how functions relate to the social construction of kinds.

For instance, consider Lackey's analysis of group belief or Bratman's of group intention. A common way of thinking about group attitudes is in terms of functionalism about mental states: group belief and group intention play functional roles in the cognitive lives of groups. Just how to understand the relation

---

[55] Millikan 1984. [56] Cummins 1975. [57] See Preston 2022.

between the functional roles and the group attitudes is a complicated matter – one might treat the attitudes as "realizations" of the functional kinds, or else one might take the functional roles to be part of what constructs the group attitudes. In either case, the membership conditions for group belief or group intention do not involve the function.

There are also cases where a kind might be thought of as functional, but where the function is a matter of causal construction – that is, the function serves in the causal explanation as to why the anchors are put in place. An example might be a legal kind, like *securities fraud*. Among the anchors for that kind might be the enactments of legislators. Those enactments ontologically socially construct the kind, but the legislators have enacted that legislation with the aim of accomplishing some function. The functional role is then a causal factor in their enacting what they do; it is part of what causally social constructs *securities fraud*. But it is (arguably) neither part of the membership conditions of securities fraud nor is it part of the ontological social construction.

In short: there are many ways functions can play a role in the membership conditions of a kind. And there are many ways a social kind can be functional even though the function does not show up in the membership conditions at all.

Material Conditions

I have already discussed material conditions, especially for racial kinds and for property, in connection with worries about psychologism. The most straightforward concerns with a psychologistic analysis of race and of property are that there seem likely to be at least some material conditions. Consider, for instance, conditions on owning something. A person owning a piece of land depends on more than simply psychological attitudes. For instance, the conditions on ownership we discussed in Section 4 involve a person physically circumnavigating a piece of land. Similarly, many racial categories may also involve material conditions, such as having a particular ancestry, a connection to a geographic location, or biological or phenotypic characteristics.

A similar, though somewhat more subtle, point might apply to group attitudes.[58] Applying the point of the last subsection, we often get material conditions if we move domain restrictions into the analysis. There are plausibly material conditions for all human kinds, since *being human* is a condition on the kind. If we recast:

---

[58] Epstein 2015, 2022.

(1a) Given any human z, z is X if and only if . . . z . . .

into

(1b) For all z, z is X if and only if z is human and . . . z . . .,

then we already have a material condition in the right-hand side. Similarly, an analysis of group belief will involve material conditions if there are material conditions on being a group. This can become a problem in discussing things like the attitudes of corporations, where the material conditions on being a corporation may figure importantly into when it is or is not appropriate to ascribe an attitude.

Some philosophers doubt these sorts of examples of material conditions for social kinds. If membership in a social kind involves meeting material conditions, the line blurs between social and nonsocial kinds. (This may or may not be a problem.) It also can be difficult to see how material conditions (rather than our knowledge or cognitive relations to those conditions) could matter for practical purposes or for social explanations.[59] This is an active area of controversy in the field.

Norms

A number of theories put norms and powers at the center of the social. We have already seen Katharine Jenkins' theory of race and gender kinds, in which their key characteristics are constraints and enablements. A number of earlier theories also regard normative features as characteristic of many or all social phenomena. John Searle, for instance, introduces the notion of "deontic powers," such as authorizations, entitlements, and rights (positive deontic powers) and requirements, obligations, and duties (negative deontic powers) (Searle 2010, p. 9). Searle argues that all "institutional facts" involve the assignment of deontic powers to nonsocial things.[60] Margaret Gilbert argues that norms arising from the formation of commitments together as a group are the hallmark of sociality.[61]

It is not altogether straightforward, however, to see how best to include norms in the conditions for being a member of a social kind. Perhaps the simplest option is to hold that social kinds are nothing different from clusters of norms. Using the simplified version of property from Section 4, here is a definition employing norms alone:

---

[59] See for instance Guala (2022) and the papers in Bulle and Di Iorio (2023a, 2023b).
[60] This is a bit crude: Searle speaks of "institutional facts" rather than kinds; and deontic powers can also be assigned iteratively to social things.
[61] Gilbert 1989.

> *Necessarily for all z, y: z owns y if and only if z has the right to exclude others from y, has the right to enclose y, has the right to use it as z wishes, and has the exclusive right to the soil and plants that grow on y.*

This is a formulation in which the conditions on ownership are exclusively normative. For something to be owned, on this analysis, is for there to be a cluster of rights and obligations associated with it. This may be ok, but it certainly is different from the formulations in the previous subsections, where there are material or psychological conditions on ownership (such as being a first occupier, or being believed to be a first occupier).

So perhaps one ought to add the material conditions: the conditions on ownership are both the material and the normative conditions. But that seems problematic too: there is a connection between the material and normative conditions. In fact, it seems as though the rights and obligations that an owner has are – at least in part – *in virtue of* the owner meeting certain material and/or psychological conditions (such as being a first occupier or being believed to be a first occupier). That would suggest the following analysis:

> *Necessarily for all z, y: z owns y if and only if z has such-and-such rights and obligations with respect to y **in virtue of (or partly in virtue of)** z having been the first to circumnavigate y.*

But this too is an odd formulation. If the norm obtains in virtue of the material fact, then it is redundant. If it obtains partly in virtue of the material fact, then we are missing a piece of analysis; and if we added that missing piece, it would again be redundant. Supposing that the missing piece is the unanimous agreement to P, this might fill out the preceding analysis:

> *Necessarily for all z, y: z owns y if and only if z has such-and-such rights and obligations with respect to y **in virtue of** (the community having unanimously agreed to P, and z having been the first to circumnavigate y).*

But if so, then we could just leave out the part about norms:

> *Necessarily for all z, y: z owns y if and only if the community unanimously agreed to P, and z was the first to circumnavigate y.*

And in that case we no longer have an account in terms of norms.

There are many ways we could go from here. Perhaps there are two different kinds – a generic kind of ownership defined in terms of norms, and a specific kind implemented in a community. (For the latter, it is not clear whether and how the norms are part of the definition of ownership.) More also needs to be said about the relation of the norms to the facts that the norms hold "in virtue of," since proposition P is probably not acceptable as is.

It seems clear that normative characteristics play an important role in social kinds. But the role they play in the definitions or analysis is not so simple as it might appear. Despite their importance, it is unclear if normative features are among the conditions for being members of a social kind, or part of the characterization or definition of the kind. In either case, it is essential to clarify the relation of norms to other components of a putative characterization.

7.2 Context

It is common for theorists to take social kinds to be restricted in their application to limited contexts, in one way or another. Here a lack of explicitness risks generating confusion.

Including Contextual Factors in the Analysis

Again using the unanimous agreement theory of property, consider the following kinds that might be constructed by that agreement:

Necessarily for all z, y: z owns y if and only if:
(a) z is the first to circumnavigate y
(b) z is the first to circumnavigate y, and z is a member of society S
(c) z is the first to circumnavigate y, and z is physically located in the site of society S
(d) z is the first to circumnavigate y, and z and y are taken by members of S to be governed by S' rules
(e) z is the first to circumnavigate y, and z is a member of society S, and all the members of S agree to proposition P.

These are just a few examples of contextual restrictions of the applicability of this case of ownership. Theories of social kinds, as stated, often look like (a), without any contextual restrictions. Sometimes that is intended. And sometimes not: implicitly the analysis is meant to be restricted. But it can be restricted in many possible ways (like (b)–(e)), so it is a problem to leave it implicit.

In filling out contextual restrictions to membership in a social kind, we need to consider shifts in the context of application – for instance, where and when and in what possibility z and y are located. Depending on the role anchors play (a point I discuss a few pages later), one might also need to consider shifts in the context of anchoring – for instance, where and when and in what possibility there is a society unanimously agreeing to proposition P (and/or similar societies and similar propositions).

For some social kinds, there may also be interesting temporal constraints on their applicability. It is a rather general principle in the law, for instance, that laws (and legal categories) do not apply retroactively. But there are certain categories that violate this: certain categories that involve horrendous crimes, for instance (such as war crimes and marital rape), are applied retroactively to instances prior to their introduction.[62]

Traveling and Local Confinement

A particularly strong kind of contextual restriction has been proposed in connection with race. Michael Root (Root 2000) argues that race "does not travel," a point that Mallon 2004 argues is central to social constructionism about race. The idea is that racial categories are confined to the cultures in which they are constructed. Mallon presents "Root's principle" as a specific instance of that constraint:[63]

> **Root's Principle:** Where R is a race, it is a necessary condition on a person being R at a site that the concept of R is used at that site to divide people.

Mallon may or may not be correct that constraints on traveling are required for socially constructed kinds. We might notice that Root's principle is not the strongest form of "no travel" constraint we might have: one could imagine that socially constructed kinds are constrained to the very sites or societies where they are constructed. So if someone moves from our society to a different one, then even if that society divides people with the same concept we do,[64] they might not fall under *our* social kind. That would be a true no-travel policy. Either of these, however, is a demanding requirement to place on socially constructed kinds; it is not clear that socially constructed kinds must be limited in this way.

It would seem, for instance, that a theory of racial and other social categories needs to make sense of categories that apply to those outside of the community (like the ancient Greek category *barbaros* to apply to non-Greeks). And to make sense categories that apply in an "etic" rather than an "emic" way, as with an anthropologist describing a culture in an ethnographic work.

Contextual restrictions are a crucial part of understanding a theory's proposed membership conditions in a kind, and warrant being stated in the analysis – that is, in the ... z ... part of (1*). To give a full characterization of a kind, any contextual restrictions – whatever they are – can be made explicit in the analysis.

---

[62] See Ticehurst (1998–1999).
[63] When combined with the thesis of "concept localism: the use of racial concepts (or some particular racial concepts) is a culturally local phenomenon" (Mallon 2004, p. 657).
[64] Mallon's "concept localism" may bear on whether concepts can be shared across sites.

Conjunctivism

In all the discussion of membership conditions, recall that we are looking for an answer to "What is X" questions, in the sense of describing *which* plain kind X corresponds to. Does it correspond to a plain kind that includes among its membership conditions being within a certain community? To a plain kind that includes certain background conditions? To a plain kind that has simple membership conditions?

A crucial but debated question is whether the anchors – the facts that socially construct the kind – are *always* among its membership conditions.[65] This seems like an abstruse question, but it is fundamental in knowing how to correctly answer "What is X" questions.

Once again to use the unanimous agreement theory of social construction applied to *property:* suppose everyone in community C agrees to proposition P. In the preceding discussion I have focused on kinds whose conditions are specified in P. Let me sidestep the question of norms I discussed a few pages back, and simply take proposition P to involve being a first occupier of land. So one option for the kind that gets socially constructed – the option I have been focusing on – is something like:

(A) *z owns y if and only if z is the first occupier of y*

But there is reason to think that this is incomplete. After all, the kind is socially constructed, and if it were not socially constructed then property would not be a social kind. So the fact that the kind was socially constructed – the fact that the anchors obtain – seems to be a required condition as well. A background condition, but still a condition. Which would make the kind, fully analyzed, have the condition:

(A+) *z owns y if and only if [(z is the first occupier of y) and (the members of z's society unanimously agree to P)]*

I have called this analysis "conjunctivist" (since it holds that the membership conditions for the kind are a conjunction of the specified conditions with the conditions on anchors), and the view that all social kinds have this form "conjunctivism."[66]

If conjunctivism is correct, then there still is a difference between the topic I have discussed in Sections 4 and 5 (i.e., the social construction) and the topic of Sections 6 and 7 (i.e., the product). It is simply that the former is a part of the

---

[65] More precisely, the conditions that the particular anchors satisfy: even if the kind is anchored by a particular set of speech acts, the particulars could be different so long as we specify the appropriate conditions.

[66] Epstein 2015, 2019a.

latter: a full account of the membership conditions of a social kind *includes* the social construction.

Why the appeal of conjunctivism? The anchors certainly seem as though they figure into the metaphysical determination of the kind. It is hard to see how that can be so if they are not among the membership conditions. If there is no ownership without the appropriate anchors, then the fact *z owns y* seems to require that the anchors (and not just first occupancy) obtain. Which makes it a condition on *z owns y* that the anchors obtain.

So why be skeptical about conjunctivism? Conjunctivism imposes a restriction on what kinds can possibly be social kinds: if you think a social kind has simple membership conditions Q, it really must have conditions Q-and-the-anchors-of-Q. For instance, you might think that the membership conditions for ownership are given by (A); but really, they are given by (A+). You might think that the conditions on group belief are those given by Lackey (see Subsection 3.2); but really, they are given by the conjunction of Lackey's conditions together with the obtaining of whatever the anchors are for group belief (agreements, functionalist ones, whatever). One might be skeptical of this restriction on possible social kinds.

Conjunctivism would also imply that a great many analyses and attempted definitions are incorrect: there are no social kinds with functional membership conditions alone, none with normative membership conditions alone, and so on. And it would mean that all social kinds are contextually restricted in specific ways, potentially ruling out things like retroactively applying kinds and kinds that apply in certain counterfactual situations.

Both sides have their challenges. But it is important, at least, to see the issue: it is common for theorists to default to conjunctivism and yet to produce analyses that are not conjunctivist. And that would appear to be inconsistent.

7.3 Departing from "If and Only If"

Now I turn from the content of the analysis of a kind to questions about the biconditional form. Earlier I pointed out that many analyses in social ontology aim to give universalized and necessitated biconditionals:

Necessarily, [for all objects z, (z is X if and only if ... z ...)]

For a long time, this was regarded as the gold standard of analyses. But actual theories of kinds in social ontology do not always take this form. There are several reasons a theorist might depart from a biconditional. One is that the theorist does not aim to give necessary and sufficient conditions. Some theories just give sufficient conditions. Others just give necessary conditions. These are both common: we sometimes aim for *less* than a necessitated biconditional.

Alternatively, we may need *more* than a necessitated biconditional, to characterize a social kind. This point arises from the recent (and ongoing) "postmodal" revolution in metaphysics. A necessitated biconditional is a modal claim about the extension of X: that is, it is a claim about the conditions for z to be X across possible worlds. (It is, of course, not required that one take talk of "possible worlds" literally.) In the last twenty years, many philosophers have questioned whether this fully captures the nature of kinds. A few papers in the literature are beginning to deal with this, especially those discussing "real definition," and it is starting to bear on discussions of social metaphysics.

Another reason we might need more than a necessitated biconditional has not gotten much attention, but I think could be as important as the others. Namely, there may be more to kinds than just membership.

In this subsection I discuss these considerations. None of it, however, is meant to suggest that we should abandon characterizations in terms of necessitated biconditionals. Even if they are no longer the gold standard, they are still a strong silver.

Partial Analyses

Some analyses only give sufficient conditions. And some only give necessary conditions. It is important to see when this happens, so that we can know what the goal of the analysis is, and what the limitations are of what is argued.

(i) Only Theorizing **Sufficient** conditions

Some accounts of social kinds do not aim to give necessary conditions for membership in the kind, but only to give sufficient conditions. An example of this is Michael Bratman's analysis of shared intention. First, he restricts his analyses to a very specific kind of group, which he calls "modestly social groups." Then, he gives a set of conditions that he argues is sufficient for that kind of group to have a shared intention. He does not argue that that is the *only* way for groups to have shared intentions. Just that it is at least one way, for at least one kind of group, to have a shared intention.

There are several reasons for his taking this strategy. Part of his aim is to demystify shared intention; that is, to argue that it *can* arise from individual intentions of group members. To accomplish this, he just needs to give a single way it can arise, not an exhaustive account. It also is already a challenge to develop a single sufficient account, so it is a worthwhile project just to address this, and to leave it to others to work on other cases and possibilities.[67]

---

[67] It is also plausible that Bratman, despite his claims, is actually aiming at more than just sufficient conditions. Some of his examples, like his Mafia case (Bratman 1993, pp. 103–4), seem to

(ii) Only Theorizing **Necessary** Conditions

Other theories in social ontology are modest in the other direction. They do not aim to give sufficient conditions, but only to defend constraints or necessary conditions for being a member of a social kind. (Or of a class of social kinds, or of all social kinds.)

We saw an example of a proposed necessary condition a few pages back, with the idea that certain kinds do not "travel." Root's argument was that racial kinds in general do not travel, and Mallon's that socially constructed kinds do not travel. Neither of these, of course, aims to give a full account of that class of kinds, but a condition they are required to meet.

Interestingly, one of the most common strategies for doing social ontology can also be understood as proposing necessary conditions: namely, ontological categorization. That is, placing a class of social entities into a broad ontological category.

Consider, for instance, the literature on the nature of social groups.[68] Most of these are proposals as to the ontological category that social groups fit into. Some hold that social groups are sets, some fusions, some pluralities, some that they are structures. These are all proposals as to the necessary conditions. (Clearly there are sets, etc., that are not social groups.) Now, some of these accounts do give sufficient conditions as well. It may be that one has done all the relevant philosophical work on the nature of groups by giving its ontological category. If all groups are sets, then, it is (arguably) straightforward to fill in remaining necessary and sufficient conditions for a particular group. But the more complex the entity – and the more complex the category it is argued to fit into – the less straightforward this is likely to be.

A large literature in social ontology, for example, focuses on artifacts, arguing that certain classes of social kinds are artifacts or artifactual kinds.[69] There is a large literature on artistic kinds, musical kinds, and fictional kinds as artifactual, and new literatures on the law as artifactual and on words as artifacts. Even if one successfully argues that one of these classes of social kinds does fall into a category like artifacts, it is clear that this is just one part of the philosophical work to be done in characterizing the kinds.

There can still be good reasons for ontological categorization. It is a familiar strategy in philosophy, closely associated with reductive projects in the

---

involve at least one necessary condition. Another possibility is that he is proposing a set of "constitutively sufficient conditions," perhaps to be understood as a set of *grounds* for a group to have a shared intention.

[68] Effingham 2010; Ritchie 2013, 2015; Hawley 2017; Strohmaier 2018; Epstein 2019b; Thomasson 2019; Horden and López de Sa 2020; Richardson 2022.

[69] Hilpinen 1993; Denkel 1995; Margolis and Laurence 2005; Thomasson 2007; Burazin 2016; Ehrenberg 2018; Irmak 2021; Preston 2022.

philosophy of science, mathematics, and mind, but with an age-old pedigree. The general aim seems to be to clear up a kind of ontological puzzlement, to say that the entities in question are nothing ontologically new or problematic, at least no more so than other things that we already know about. We may still debate the characteristics of the broad category. But if we know that a class of social kinds all fit into a given category, then we do not need to worry about the ontology status of that class any more than we do about the category as a whole. Another aim of categorization is to get some new perspective or insight into why the entities in question have the features they do. If we know that laws are artifacts, and we know that artifacts are all individuated in some general ways, then laws inherit those ways.

Part of the problem with these literatures, on the other hand, is that ontological categories are often just as ill-understood as classes of social kinds. And it is devilishly hard to argue conclusively for one category rather than another. In the literature on the nature of words, for instance, philosophers have been arguing for years among a wide range of possible ontological categories: words are types, words are continuants, words are type-continuants, words are shape-forms, words are species, words are artifacts, words are representations, words are abstract artifacts, words are positions in structures, words are property clusters, words are fictions, and so on.[70] One starts to get the sense that while many of these are informative heuristics for modeling words, there is little basis for deciding on a particular one.

Criticism aside, though, the point is that many projects and vibrant debates in social ontology are not focused on providing a necessitated universalized biconditional, but rather on a portion of it.

(iii) If Social Kinds Do Not Have Determinate Membership Conditions

Another possibility is that biconditionals are too much to demand because social kinds do not have determinate extensions or sets of membership conditions. A full analysis of a social kind will fall short of a necessitated universalized biconditional.

Notice that this is different from the claim that social kinds are dynamic, or even constantly in flux. A dynamic picture of kinds is compatible with there being determinate membership conditions at any given time and/or context. But determinacy can be questioned as well (see Section 8).

More than Biconditionals

It is not easy to give necessary and sufficient conditions for membership in a kind. One should not doubt that that is a high bar. Yet there are reasons for

---

[70] See, for instance, Kaplan 1990; Cappelen 1999; Alward 2005; Epstein 2009; Hawthorne and Lepore 2011; Irmak 2019; Nefdt 2019; Miller 2021.

thinking that it is not enough: we may want more than a necessitated universalized biconditional.

There are two reasons for this. One comes out of a new way of thinking about the nature of things and their relation to one another – a field that, for the lack of a better name, is currently known as "post-modal metaphysics." The other is a reason I think deserves attention – that there can be more to a kind than its membership conditions.

(i) Post-modal Considerations: More to z Being X than a Biconditional

The idea of a necessitated universalized biconditional, again, is to give necessary and sufficient conditions for any object, across any possibility, to be member of that kind. To say that this is a complete characterization of the kind X implies that kinds are *individuated* by these conditions. If you have a kind X_1 and a kind X_2 that have the same such conditions, then X_1 and X_2 are the same kind.

There has long been reason, however, to doubt this. A widely discussed case comes from Plato's *Euthyphro*, which considers the argument as to whether an act is pious because it is loved by the gods, or whether it is loved by the gods because it is pious. The pious acts are exactly the same acts as those that are loved by the gods. Yet *being pious* is not the same thing as *being loved by the gods*. Otherwise it would not make sense to ask which one is because of the other. A number of philosophers argue that similar considerations apply to a range of social kinds.

Another (closely related) reason to be dissatisfied with biconditionals is that it seems that there are sources or explanations for the necessitated universalized biconditionals to hold. It seems odd that a complete account of a kind like property or race or group belief could be given with a list of its actual and possible members. But rather that there must be a deeper reason for its membership conditions to hold, and that that reason is not the same as the enumeration of the members.

Philosophers have taken several approaches to these considerations in the last few years. The notion of *grounding* is being applied to a number of problems in social ontology (Epstein 2015, Schaffer 2017, Griffith 2018), and there is a growing neo-Aristotelian literature on *essence* being applied to social entities (Koslicki 2008, Fine 2020, Passinsky 2021).

And there is an interesting new literature on "real definition." Rosen (2015), Fine (2015), and Correia and Skiles (2019), for instance, all give accounts of real definition that draw on both ground and essence. (Though this literature does not yet engage much with the social.)

Others are skeptical of these cases, arguing that kinds are not individuated as finely as some post-modal theorists hold, but that the phenomena can be accounted for using linguistic and representational considerations. (In connection with this and the real definition literature, see the recent literature on generalized identity, including Rayo 2013 and Dorr 2016).

(ii) More to the Nature of X than z Being X

I want to propose a different reason that an answer to "what is X" questions demand more than biconditionals as answers. This reason is also distinct from the post-modal considerations I just discussed. There is an assumption which has been baked into the inquiry for definition and analysis of kinds – an assumption that was made by Socrates and still holds enormous sway.

Specifically, the question "what is X?" has been interpreted as – collapsed into – the question "what is it for something to be an X?"[71] This interpretation is built into Plato's approach to definition.[72] And – to jump 2,500 years – it is assumed in contemporary papers on real definition. Gideon Rosen, in "Real Definition," asserts the equivalence explicitly:

> To answer the question "What is courage?" ... is to say what it is for a person to be courageous – to identify that in which the courage of the courageous person consists – by specifying non-trivial necessary and sufficient conditions for courage somehow grounded in the nature of courage itself. (Rosen 2015, p. 189)

And the same assumption is made in other recent discussions of real definition, including the ones I mentioned earlier – Fine (2015), Correia and Skiles (2019) – and the recent literature on generalized identity.[73]

This long-standing assumption, I propose, is mistaken. The two questions are not the same: one can give a full account of what it is for something to be X, and yet not exhaust the nature of X itself. This suggests a claim about the individuation of kinds: there can be two kinds that receive the same answer to "what is it for something to be X" but that are nonetheless distinct kinds.

What else can be part of the nature of a kind X, apart from what it is to be an X? If one rejects conjunctivism (as I do), then there may be countless features

---

[71] Dan López de Sa and I call this "predicational equivalence"; this subsection is informed by our joint work on the topic.

[72] In *Meno*, Plato argues that answers to "What is X" questions involve giving an account of the one thing in virtue of which all cases of X are X, and the knowing of which enables one to distinguish something that is X from something that is not (*Meno*, 72c7-d1; Charles 2010, pp. 5–6).

[73] There was a brief debate between Correia and Fine on whether there is a difference between "objectual essences" and "predicational essences," but the debate turned on different issues than the present concern, and resulted in both parties taking a predicational approach (see Correia 2006, Fine 2015).

that are. On a pluralist theory of social construction, for instance, a kind with a given set of membership conditions could be constructed in more than one way. If the way a kind is constructed is essential to it, then two kinds have different essences, despite "what it is for something be X" being the same. (For instance, if kinds can be constructed by convention and also can be constructed via regularities that support inductive explanation, there might be two kinds that are distinct because they were constructed these two ways, despite the kinds having the same membership conditions.)

Something else that can be part of the nature of a kind, apart from its membership conditions, is normative properties. Kinds might, for instance, be constructed with strictly material membership conditions, but where members essentially also have normative properties. This is a promising way we could deal with the problem of the norms associated with ownership, which we discussed in Subsection 7.1. On this approach, the conditions for ownership could be given exhaustively by first occupancy, but it would also be essential to ownership that anything satisfying its conditions would also have certain rights and obligations.

Even one who accepts conjunctivism can find ways the assumption is mistaken. It may be that some kinds are essentially natural, or essentially fundamental, while others are not. Or the kind as a whole may have normative features that are not reflected in its membership.

There is much more to be said and argued on this topic. Overturning the long-standing commitment to the Socratic equivalence of "what is X" and "what is it for something to be X" is not to be taken lightly. But it is intriguing: close scrutiny of social kinds may lead us to revise long-standing assumptions and models about the nature of the world more generally.

7.4 Analyzing Social Kinds in General

The more ambitious theorizing in social ontology aims to explain or analyze *large classes* of social kinds, or even social kinds *in general*. One way to think about these theories – at least many of them – is that they propose that there is a subclass of "plain kinds" which exhausts all of the kinds that can possibly be social kinds.

Strict psychologism, for instance, holds that membership in any social kind is ontologically determined by – and only by – psychological properties of individual people. So the set of possible social kinds corresponds to (or corresponds to a subset of) the plain kinds whose membership conditions involve psychological properties of individual people. Functionalism about all social kinds involves the set of possible social kinds corresponding to (or corresponding to a subset of) the plain kinds whose membership conditions are causal roles (or however the theory interprets functions). Or if one holds that all social kinds involve certain sorts of norms, then the candidate social kinds correspond to (or correspond to a subset of) the plain kinds with those norms. While this is a fairly obvious point, it still helps highlight the need for a theorist not just to generalize about the kinds within that class, but to account for the exclusion of all other kinds from the set of possible or candidate social kinds.

Other theories of social kinds generalize about social construction – that *all* social kinds must be constructed in a particular way – and implicitly endorse "conjunctivism," taking the conditions on social construction to be among the conditions on membership in the kind. So again, these views can be seen as restricting the possible social kinds to a subset of the plain kinds: only the plain kinds with conditions like *Q and the society unanimously agrees to Q*, for instance, would be among the possible social kinds.

This is a strong claim for a theory to make: that there are no possible social kinds that do not meet the proposed conditions. Some general theories presumably want to do less, perhaps claiming that the proposed class is an important class of social kinds. In that case, it is incumbent on the theorist to explain what is important about that class in comparison to others.

8 Pulling It Together: Social Kinds and Social Construction

The approach to social ontology in this Element has been to focus on social kinds and then to divide the inquiry in two parts – what *constructs* social kinds, and how to characterize the *resulting* kinds. But of course, these are parts of a single package. A theory of social construction is accountable to a theory of social kinds, and vice versa: a good theory will explain how social construction works and also what gets constructed.

I have put this two-part inquiry as a model for clarifying and answering questions in social ontology, including a variety of things we might take "what is X" questions to be asking. I have focused on ontological questions (since that, after all, is the topic the field focuses on), but there are other ways of construing and answering such questions as well. And this two-part model is just a model: it allows that the parts can overlap, and it does not rule out other ways of apportioning the inquiry.

Even though the inquiries bear on one another, it is entirely reasonable to pursue just one part or aspect of the projects in the field. We have a great deal of experience navigating the social world, and on this basis one can develop a theory of a particular social kind (or other entity) without needing a theory of the social world as a whole. Still, we need to understand that a full theory involves all the parts, and that in the community's inquiry into social ontology theories need to be weighed in light of one another.

In Sections 4 and 5 I discussed theories of social construction, and in Sections 6 and 7 theories of the products of construction, by way of theorizing about the analysis of social kinds. But there are still crucial missing pieces: I have said that we can think of the "product" of social construction as being putting in place the sticking out of a social kind (or set of social kinds), but apart from examples, have not talked systematically about how to interpret sticking out. Nor have I really addressed the connection between theories of social construction and its products: I have only stated that it is a desideratum for these theories that they show how the anchors (or the things that do the construction work) ontologically result in the social kind sticking out.

The main reason for this is that the field is wide open. In this section I will briefly comment on potential approaches to sticking out and what social construction accomplishes. But this is largely programmatic, since most of the work on this topic has yet to be done.

And then I will return to projects in social ontology more generally, connecting some of the themes from Section 1 to the inquiries discussed in the following sections.

8.1 Sticking Out and What Social Construction Accomplishes

In discussing the unanimous agreement theory of social construction, I suggested a way of thinking about what unanimous agreement accomplishes – that is, how that sort of social construction purports to make a kind stick out. Unanimous agreement to a proposition P, the theory might hold, makes the norms stated in P *binding* for us. And social kinds stick out, according to the theory, exactly in that they involve norms that we are bound by. That was just a quick idea, and in later discussion I raised a number of problems with the idea that unanimous agreement does bind us, with formulating such a proposition P, and with norms (especially as membership conditions).

I also raised a number of other ways a theorist might regard social kinds as "sticking out." Many discussions, as we have seen, aim to explain the existence of social kinds, some using the same machinery as in widespread explanations of the existence of natural kinds, some using different machinery. And I have listed a variety of families of theories of social construction, many of which come along with their own theories of what makes a social kind exist or otherwise stick out.

How do we think about this topic – namely, what it is for a kind to be distinctive and how a theory of social construction might account for the determination of distinctiveness? One model we might go back to is to start with an abundant space of plain kinds. Then we can ask, what is it that, given that space, social construction does? If we start with the view that all the plain kinds *exist,* then there are two options regarding the sticking-out kinds. Either the sticking-out kinds are a subset of the plain kinds, in which case social construction cannot be making-kinds-exist, since all the plain kinds already exist. Or the sticking-out kinds might correspond to – but are not identical to – the plain kinds, in which case social construction *could be* making the sticking-out kinds exist.

Or we could start with the view that the plain kinds do not all exist. In which case, social construction might be making certain plain kinds exist. Or the other alternatives are also available: it could be making other things exist, things that correspond to but are not identical to plain kinds. Or it could be that the sticking out of social kinds is not to be understood in terms of their existence.

If not in terms of existence, maybe sticking out is a matter of a plain kind having a contingent property, like being represented, or being apt to serve in inductive explanations. In that case, we might think of social construction as making it the case that some plain kind has that contingent property. So a complete theory of social construction would account for any way that the plain kind's having the relevant property could be ontologically determined.

Interestingly, things look a little different for the conjunctivist about social kinds (see Subsection 7.2). For a conjunctivist, not all plain kinds are eligible to be social kinds. Instead, a general theory of social construction specifies a subset of the plain kinds that are (or that correspond to) the *possible* social kinds. For instance (as we discussed earlier), it may be that the only possible social kinds are those whose conditions are of the form: *(Q) and the society unanimously agree to Q.* To socially construct a kind, then, is just to make the world satisfy part of the conditions of that kind. In that case, the sense that social construction makes that kind stick out should be understood as something like making that kind locally instantiable; that is, putting in place the background conditions that makes satisfaction of the foreground conditions sufficient for kind membership.

These are a few initial directions one might pursue in investigating the connection between social construction and what it yields – the social kinds it yields and what (if anything) is special about them.

8.2 Assumptions and Aims of Social Ontology

On some models of social kinds, they are immutable, fixed once and for all time. Even socially constructed kinds may be immutable: a kind is constructed to have certain membership conditions and/or other features, and that is what the kind is. If a kind is constructed with different features, even ones quite similar to the other, it is a different kind.

This may be the way kinds are, or may be a good model to work with, but nothing I have said in this Element assumes that social kinds are stable. The identity conditions of social kinds might permit them to be malleable: their membership conditions might change, with kinds re-anchored dynamically. They might even be extremely fluid, shifting conditions in different contexts. They might shift in processes of "metalinguistic negotiation," where terms can change their meanings as we push and pull how they are to be understood, and the representations then figuring into the anchoring of the kinds themselves. It is also possible (perhaps likely) that if kinds can be made to stick out, they can also lose their sticking-out-ed-ness; if they can be brought into existence, they can also cease to exist.

All this malleability is still compatible with determinacy. Even if a kind can change – perhaps even radically – from time to time and from situation to situation, it still might be that they have determinate membership conditions and other features. In this Element I have not assumed any degree of stability (though I have considered proposals regarding social construction that do presuppose certain sorts of stability). But I have been working with a model where kinds are taken to be determinate. I have repeatedly used the model in which a social kind corresponds to one particular plain kind, where plain kinds are taken to have determinate extensions across possible worlds. In discussing departures from necessitated universalized biconditionals, I have mostly discussed ways they are *at least* as determinate as this: I have mentioned post-modal approaches, where giving the real definition of a kind involves more texture than the biconditionals, and regarding analyses that give us less than biconditionals, I have called them "partial" or "incomplete" analyses.

Perhaps we should abandon this assumption too. It is plausible social kinds are not just malleable, but also indeterminate in various ways. It may be, for instance, that there is simply no fact of the matter about the extension of a kind outside a process of metalinguistic negotiation, and that the negotiation only resolves a small bit of indeterminacy.

A number of theorists have also recently argued against the project of seeking a descriptive characterization of social kinds altogether. One way to pursue a critical project is to characterize a social kind and to give an account of how it has been socially constructed, and then to criticize either or both. Some social kinds are "vicious" – that is, have oppressive consequences – while other are "rotten" – that is, have oppressive anchors. Rotten categories may be problematic even if they are not vicious. (See Epstein 2010). A different approach rejects this two-step process of doing the social ontology "neutrally" and then using the results to critique. Instead this approach holds that such a characterization has normative assumptions and/or consequences, and hence that characterization should itself be *ameliorative*. (See Haslanger 2012, Jenkins 2016, Dutilh Novaes 2020, Marques forthcoming).

The field of social ontology also tends to assume that it makes sense to do ontology – that it makes sense to ask about the nature of social entities in some sense, and that some sort of philosophical analysis is pertinent to addressing such questions. This also is a topic of debate and theorizing (see for instance Lauer 2019, Hindriks and Guala 2023, Ross 2023).

There are a great many avenues for exploration. As I said at the outset, we should not overestimate the significance of philosophical inquiry for any practical task: there are many disciplines that bear on understanding, assessment, and improvement of the social world. But social ontology does hold promise. And it is complicated and fascinating.

References

Alward, P. (2005). Between the Lines of Age: Reflections on the Metaphysics of Words. *Pacific Philosophical Quarterly*, 86, 172–87.

Appiah, A. (1985). The Uncompleted Argument: Du Bois and the Illusion of Race. *Critical Inquiry*, 12(1), 21–37.

Ásta (2018). *Categories We Live By: The Construction of Sex, Gender, Race, and Other Social Categories*. Oxford: Oxford University Press.

Attwood, B. (2020). *Empire and the Making of Native Title: Sovereignty, Property and Indigenous People*. Cambridge: Cambridge University Press.

Bird, A. and E. Tobin (2023). *Natural Kinds*. The Stanford Encyclopedia of Philosophy (Spring 2023 Edition).

Boyd, R. (1999). *Homeostasis, Species, and Higher Taxa*. In R. Wilson (Ed.), Species: New Interdisciplinary Essays (pp. 141–85). Cambridge, MA: MIT Press.

Bratman, M. (1993). Shared Intention. *Ethics*, 104(1), 97–113.

(2014). *Shared Agency*. Oxford: Oxford University Press.

Bulle, N. and F. Di Iorio (2023a). *The Palgrave Handbook of Methodological Individualism: Volume I*. Cham, Switzerland: Springer Verlag.

(2023b). *The Palgrave Handbook of Methodological Individualism: Volume II*. Cham, Switzerland: Springer Verlag.

Burazin, L. (2016). Can There Be an Artifact Theory of Law? *Ratio Juris*, 29(3), 385–401.

Burman, Å. (2023). *Nonideal Social Ontology: The Power View*. New York: Oxford University Press.

Cappelen, H. (1999). Intentions in Words. *Noûs*, 33(1), 92–102.

Charles, D. (2010). *Definition in Greek Philosophy*. New York: Oxford University Press.

Collins, S. (2019). *Group Duties: Their Existence and Their Implications for Individuals*. Oxford, UK: Oxford University Press.

Correia, F. (2006). Generic Essence, Objectual Essence, and Modality. *Noûs*, 40(4), 753–67.

Correia, F. and A. Skiles (2019). Grounding, Essence, and Identity. *Philosophy and Phenomenological Research*, 98(3), 642–70.

Cummins, R. E. (1975). Functional Analysis. *Journal of Philosophy*, 72(20), 741–64.

Denkel, A. (1995). Artifacts and Constituents. *Philosophy and Phenomenological Research*, 55(2), 311–22.

Dorr, C. (2016). To Be F Is To Be G. *Philosophical Perspectives*, 30(1), 39–134.
Dutilh Novaes, C. (2020). Carnapian Explication and Ameliorative Analysis: A Systematic Comparison. *Synthese*, 197(3), 1011–34.
Effingham, N. (2010). The Metaphysics of Groups. *Philosophical Studies*, 149(2), 251–67.
Ehrenberg, K. M. (2018). Law is an Institution an Artifact and a Practice. In L. Burazin, K. E. Himma and C. Roversi (Eds.), *Law as an Artifact* (pp. 177–91): Oxford, UK: Oxford University Press.
Epstein, B. (2009). Grounds, Convention, and the Metaphysics of Linguistic Tokens. *Croatian Journal of Philosophy*, 9(25), 45–67.
  (2010). History and the Critique of Social Concepts. *Philosophy of the Social Sciences*, 40(1), 3–29.
  (2013). Social Objects without Intentions. In A. Konzelmann Ziv and H. B. Schmid (Eds.), *Institutions, Emotions, and Group Agents: Contributions to Social Ontology* (pp. 53–68). Dordrecht: Springer.
  (2014). How Many Kinds of Glue Hold the Social World Together? In M. Galloti and J. Michael (Eds.), *Perspectives on Social Ontology and Social Cognition* (pp. 41–55). Dordrecht: Springer.
  (2015). *The Ant Trap: Rebuilding the Foundations of the Social Sciences*. New York: Oxford University Press.
  (2019a). Anchoring versus Grounding: Reply to Schaffer. *Philosophy and Phenomenological Research*, 99(3), 768–81.
  (2019b). What are Social Groups? Their Metaphysics and How to Classify Them. *Synthese*, 196, 4899–932.
  (2022). Why Group Mental States are Not Exhaustively Determined by Member States. *Philosophical Issues*, 32(1), 417–33.
Fine, K. (2015). Unified Foundations for Essence and Ground. *Journal of the American Philosophical Association*, 1(2), 296–311.
  (2020). The Identity of Social Groups. *Metaphysics*, 3(1), 81–91.
Geertz, C. (1973). *The Interpretation of Cultures: Selected Essays*. New York: Basic Books.
Gilbert, M. (1989). *On Social Facts*. Princeton: Princeton University Press.
  (1990). Walking Together: A Paradigmatic Social Phenomenon. *Midwest Studies in Philosophy*, 15, 1–14.
  (2014). *Joint Commitment*. Oxford: Oxford University Press.
Griffith, A. M. (2018). Social Construction and Grounding. *Philosophy and Phenomenological Research*, 97(2), 393–409.
Guala, F. (2016). Epstein on Anchors and Grounds. *Journal of Social Ontology*, 2(1), 135–47.

(2022). Rescuing Ontological Individualism. *Philosophy of Science*, 89(3), 471–85.

Gupta, A. and S. Mackereth (2023). *Definitions*. The Stanford Encyclopedia of Philosophy (Fall 2023 Edition).

Hacking, I. (1999). *The Social Construction of What?* Cambridge, MA: Harvard University Press.

Hardimon, M. O. (2017). *Rethinking Race: The Case for Deflationary Realism*. Harvard University Press.

Haslanger, S. (1995). Ontology and Social Construction. *Philosophical Topics*, 23, 95–125.

Haslanger, S. (2012). *Resisting Reality: Social Construction and Social Critique*. Oxford University Press.

(2016). Theorizing with a Purpose: The Many Kinds of Sex. In C. Kendig (Ed.), *Natural Kinds and Classification in Scientific Practice* (pp. 129–44). London: Routledge.

Hawley, K. (2017). Social Mereology. *Journal of the American Philosophical Association*, 3(4), 395–411.

(2019). Comments on Brian Epstein's The Ant Trap. *Inquiry*, 62(2), 217–29.

Hawthorne, J. and E. Lepore (2011). On Words. *Journal of Philosophy*, 108(9), 447–85.

Hilpinen, R. (1993). Authors and Artifacts. *Proceedings of the Aristotelian Society*, 93, 155–78.

Hindriks, F. and F. Guala (2023). The Nature and Significance of Social Ontology. *Synthese*, 201(4), 1–22.

Horden, J. and D. López de Sa (2020). Groups as Pluralities. *Synthese*, 198(11), 10237–71.

Huebner, B. (2013). *Macrocognition: A Theory of Distributed Minds and Collective Intentionality*. New York: Oxford University Press.

Irmak, N. (2019). An Ontology of Words. *Erkenntnis*, 84(5), 1139–58.

(2021). The Problem of Creation and Abstract Artifacts. *Synthese*, 198(10), 9695–708.

Jenkins, K. (2016). Amelioration and Inclusion: Gender Identity and the Concept of Woman. *Ethics*, 126(2), 394–421.

(2023). *Ontology and Oppression: Race, Gender, and Social Reality*. New York: Oxford University Press.

Jones, J.-E. (2023). *Locke on Real Essence*. The Stanford Encyclopedia of Philosophy (Summer 2023 Edition).

Kaplan, D. (1990). Words. *Proceedings of the Aristotelian Society*, 64, 93–119.

Khalidi, M. A. (2013). Three Kinds of Social Kinds. *Philosophy and Phenomenological Research*, 90(1), 96–112.

Koslicki, K. (2008). *The Structure of Objects*. Oxford: Oxford University Press.

Lackey, J. (2021). *The Epistemology of Groups*. Oxford: Oxford University Press.

Lauer, R. (2019). Is Social Ontology Prior to Social Scientific Methodology? *Philosophy of the Social Sciences*, 49(3), 171–89.

List, C. and P. Pettit (2011). *Group Agency: The Possibility, Design, and Status of Corporate Agents*. Oxford: Oxford University Press.

Magnus, P. D. (2015). John Stuart Mill on Taxonomy and Natural Kinds. *Hopos: The Journal of the International Society for the History of Philosophy of Science*, 5(2), 269–80.

Mallon, R. (2004). Passing, Traveling and Reality: Social constructionism and the metaphysics of race. *Noûs*, 38(4), 644–73.

(2016). *The Construction of Human Kinds*. Oxford: Oxford University Press.

Margolis, E. and S. Laurence (Eds.) (2005). *Creations of the Mind: Essays on Artifacts and their Representation*. Oxford: Oxford University Press.

Marques, T. (forthcoming). Representing or Shaping Reality? What "Class" can Teach about "Woman". In M. G. Isaac, S. Koch and K. Scharp (Eds.), *New Perspectives on Conceptual Engineering*: Cham, Switzerland: Springer.

McPherson, L. (2024). *The Afterlife of Race: An Informed Philosophical Search*. New York: Oxford University Press.

Miller, J. T. M. (2021). Words, Species, and Kinds. *Metaphysics*, 4(1), 18–31.

Millikan, R. G. (1984). *Language, Thought, and Other Biological Categories: New Foundations for Realism*. Cambridge, MA: MIT Press.

Nefdt, R. M. (2019). The Ontology of Words: A Structural Approach. *Inquiry: An Interdisciplinary Journal of Philosophy*, 62(8), 877–911.

Pagano, E. (2023). Social Construction, Social Kinds and Exportation. *Analysis*, 84(1), 83–93.

Passinsky, A. (2021). Finean Feminist Metaphysics. *Inquiry: An Interdisciplinary Journal of Philosophy*, 64(9), 937–54.

Preston, B. (2022). *Artifact*. The Stanford Encyclopedia of Philosophy (Winter 2022 Edition).

Rayo, A. (2013). *The Construction of Logical Space*. Oxford, UK: Oxford University Press.

Richardson, K. (2022). Social Groups are Concrete Material Particulars. *Canadian Journal of Philosophy*, 52(4), 468–483

Ritchie, K. (2013). What are Groups? *Philosophical Studies*, 166(2), 257–72.

(2015). The Metaphysics of Social Groups. *Philosophy Compass*, 10(5), 310–21.

Root, M. (2000). How We Divide the World. *Philosophy of Science*, 67(3), 639.

Rosen, G. (2015). Real Definition. *Analytic Philosophy*, 56(3), 189–209.

Ross, D. (2023). Scientific Metaphysics and Social Science. *Synthese*, 202(5), 1–34.

Roth, A. S. (2023). The Stability of Social Categories. *European Journal of Philosophy*, 31(1), 297–309.

Ryle, G. (1968). *The Thinking of Thoughts: What is "Le Penseur" Doing?*, Collected Papers, Volume 2 (pp. 480–96). London: Hutchinson.

Schaffer, J. (2017). Social Construction as Grounding; Or: Fundamentality for Feminists, a Reply to Barnes and Mikkola. *Philosophical Studies*, 174(10), 2449–65.

(2019). Anchoring as Grounding: On Epstein's the Ant Trap. *Philosophy and Phenomenological Research*, 99(3), 749–67.

Schmid, H. B. (2023). *We, Together: The Social Ontology of Us*. New York: Oxford University Press.

Searle, J. R. (1990). Collective Intentions and Actions. In P. Cohen, J. Morgan and M. E. Pollack (Eds.), *Intentions in Communication* (pp. 401–415). Cambridge, MA: Bradford Books.

(1998). Social Ontology and the Philosophy of Society. *Analyse & Kritik*, 20(2), 143–58.

(2010). *Making the Social World: The Structure of Human Civilization*. Oxford: Oxford University Press.

Strohmaier, D. (2018). Group Membership and Parthood. *Journal of Social Ontology*, 4(2), 121–35.

Thomasson, A. (2007). Artifacts and Human Concepts. In E. Margolis and S. Laurence (Eds.), *Creations of the Mind: Theories of Artifacts and their Representation* (52–73). Oxford: Oxford University Press.

(2019). The Ontology of Social Groups. *Synthese*, 196(12), 4829–45.

Ticehurst, R. (1998–1999). Retroactive Criminal Law. *King's College Law Journal*, 9, 88–108.

Tollefsen, D. (2015). *Groups as Agents*. Cambridge, MA: Polity.

Tuomela, R. (2013). *Social Ontology*. Oxford: Oxford University Press.

Tuomela, R. and K. Miller (1988). We-Intentions. *Philosophical Studies*, 53(3), 367–89.

Williams, B. (1981). *Ethics and the Limits of Philosophy*. Cambridge, MA: Harvard University Press.

Acknowledgments

I am grateful to many people for their help and support with this and related projects. The Tufts Philosophy Department has been an ideal environment for research, and I am also grateful to Tufts for sabbatical support, and to Avner Baz for encouraging me to write this Element. I am grateful to Tuomas Tahko for his support, as well as his patience with ever-extending deadlines.

I also want to express my appreciation to the many people I have worked with in recent years on broad topics in social ontology. In particular, discussions with Dan López de Sa, Asya Passinsky, and Johan Brannmark have been a lifeline in the last few years. I also would like to thank Sally Haslanger, François Schroeter, Muhammad Ali Khalidi, and an anonymous referee, as well as participants at colloquia at the University of Melbourne, Monash University, the University of Sydney, the University of Wollongong, the ANU, and at Social Ontology 2024 held at Duke University.

As ever, my greatest debt is to my family – to Gabriel and Lily, who make each day a joy, and to Sarah, walking hand in hand through it all.

Cambridge Elements

Metaphysics

Tuomas E. Tahko
University of Bristol

Tuomas E. Tahko is Professor of Metaphysics of Science at the University of Bristol, UK. Tahko specialises in contemporary analytic metaphysics, with an emphasis on methodological and epistemic issues: 'meta-metaphysics'. He also works at the interface of metaphysics and philosophy of science: 'metaphysics of science'. Tahko is the author of *Unity of Science* (Cambridge University Press, 2021, *Elements in Philosophy of Science*), *An Introduction to Metametaphysics* (Cambridge University Press, 2015), and editor of *Contemporary Aristotelian Metaphysics* (Cambridge University Press, 2012).

About the Series

This highly accessible series of Elements provides brief but comprehensive introductions to the most central topics in metaphysics. Many of the Elements also go into considerable depth, so the series will appeal to both students and academics. Some Elements bridge the gaps between metaphysics, philosophy of science, and epistemology.

Cambridge Elements

Metaphysics

Elements in the Series

Chemistry's Metaphysics
Vanessa A. Seifert

Ontological Categories: A Methodological Guide
Katarina Perovic

Abstract Objects
David Liggins

Grounding, Fundamentality and Ultimate Explanations
Ricki Bliss

Metaphysics and the Sciences
Matteo Morganti

Teleology
Matthew Tugby

Modal Naturalism: Science and the Modal Facts
Amanda Bryant, Alastair Wilson

Metaphysics of Race
Kal H. Kalewold

Metaphysics of Causation
Max Kistler

The Metaphysics of Gender
E. Díaz León

Reduction, Emergence and the Metaphysics in Science
Carl Gillett

Social Ontology
Brian Epstein

A full series listing is available at: www.cambridge.org/EMPH

For EU product safety concerns, contact us at Calle de José Abascal, 56–1°, 28003 Madrid, Spain or eugpsr@cambridge.org

www.ingramcontent.com/pod-product-compliance
Lightning Source LLC
LaVergne TN
LVHW020351260326
834688LV00045B/1653